Scotland as We Know It

project is trying to accomplish: locating over a century's worth of Scottish national and cultural identity within its incredibly diffuse and elusive manifestations. We can imagine that for Stein, it was not that Oakland had disappeared, but that the images, myths and fictions of Oakland were inadequate accounts of the reality she experienced there: her there was not "the" there. For my analysis of nation the trick is not find out what is "really" there, but to discover how the different "theres" are ideologically constructed and enabled in competing for institutional and political legitimacy as their effects are felt on an everyday basis. Scotland is indeed there, but as this book shows, it takes more than a few fingers to point to it.

Chapter One

SCOTTISH NATIONALITY AND TARTAN CULTURE

In 1953, Forsyth Hardy, a *Scotsman* film critic and long-time advocate for the Scottish film industry, was visited by a Hollywood producer looking for a site to film the motion picture version of the Broadway musical *Brigadoon*. Starring Gene Kelly and Cyd Charisse, the cinema musical set in a Highland village needed to be filmed somewhere particularly Scottish. After searching various locations across the Highland countryside, the producer, Arthur Freed, concluded that none of the small communities he visited lived up to the portrait of idyllic quaintness he had expected. Freed finally opted to build his set for *Brigadoon* on the MGM lot in Culver City, California: "'I went to Scotland,' he said, 'but I could find nothing that looked like Scotland.'"[1] As his words reveal, the filmmaker was not looking for Scotland itself— after all, he was standing in the middle of it — but for something that resembled what he wanted Scotland to be: a dream world of pre-industrial crofting villages, peculiar folk customs, and thickly accented happy farmers.

I begin with this oft-cited story because it reflects a common position of Scottish culture within modern conceptions of Anglo-American nationality. Represented repeatedly as a culturally backward, but unadulterated ancient land of Europe, agrarian Scotland and its Highlands have served as an imaginative reserve for responding to contemporary anxieties about modernity, Empire, and social change. Portrayals of Scotland, by Scots and non–Scots alike, in modern literature, film, and popular culture have been, and continue to be, rife with popular exotic images of a harmonious pre-modern national culture. Once regarded as backwards and coarse denizens of a primitive world, Highlanders, as well as agrarian workers and fishers from the lowland and Western Isles, were transformed by an international elite into brave and virile warriors, bonnie lasses, docile laborers, melancholic folk, proud orderly clans, and many combinations of these. The countryside stood in for an ongoing fantasy of better times almost always linked to an organically arranged social world of peace, beauty, cooperation, honor, and cultural purpose. As fantasies throughout the last century, they have provided not only a psychological escape from contemporary reality, but also from the history of Scotland itself, which clearly identifies them as modern inventions. But more than mere escape or the result of overactive imagination, these images of auld Scotland draw ideological lines around deeply-held views about contested social issues of family, work, citizenship, gender roles, racial privileges, and so forth? From the 18th century onwards, with the work of Sir Walter Scott, James Macpherson's *Ossian*, and the Stuarts' cultivated infatuation with a sanitized version of the Scottish character, these images of Scotland continue to reveal a longing for origins that provide particular meanings to a variety of social practices, including rallies for cultural sovereignty and attempts to build political communities. Uncomplicated representations of wholeness and social permanence deflect and compensate for feelings of cultural loss and isolation. Often they inhabit the guise of historical truths that are nostalgically celebrated and reenacted. At other times, these images of the Scottish past serve as a lightning rod for passionate and important critiques aimed at the dangers of sentimentalized histories and the inevitably oppressive elision of difference contained in such discourses of essential unity. In each case, the same Scotland that *Brigadoon*'s American film producer was looking for, and ultimately manufactured on his own, has loomed like a specter in depictions of Scotland, particularly in the last one and a half centuries. Whole literary schools, social organizations, nationalist political movements, and tourist economies have been inspired or cursed by the ghost of the pre-modern Scot. Through intricate and shifting means, this vision appears as either the warm return of an old friend or the grotesque ramblings of a tartan-clad monster.

Expressions of Scottish nationality since the late nineteenth century have been particularly invested in constructing the physical, emotional, and social characteristics of male subjectivity. It is during this period that Scotland became fully initiated as a *cultural* community of its own rather than a regional flavor or a socially undeveloped space within the British Isles. Matthew Arnold's famous 1866 treatise *On the Study of Celtic Literature* posed Scotland (along with Wales and Ireland) as a primary model, as well as a problem, in defining, maintaining and preserving marginal cultural identity.[2] Scotland's local practices, language, writing, music, even temperament, according to Arnold, demonstrated that Scottish ways were much more than a derivative phenomenon of British civilization, but an identifiable and coherent unit recognizable through its own distinctive, albeit inferior, arts and expressions. Scotland possessed an aesthetic tradition to be studied, documented, and observed, but only as it could be sustained as a relic by a more enlightened public, functioning as a material resource for the elevation of more evolved traditions like those found in England. One might say that Arnold's conjuration of "Celtic nature," its arts, language and poetry in 1866, serves as a prelude to the subsequent legacy surrounding Scottish representation. Scots, Irish, and Welsh, Arnold argues, are an essential limb to the "English empire" since "we are deeply interested in knowing them, they are deeply interested in being known by us."[3] Like *Brigadoon*, Scotland's cultural reality seems to exist only when it is consumed, produced, and reproduced from elsewhere. Arnold was not alone in his qualified enthusiasm for Scotland's cultural artifacts. The late nineteenth century's "Celtic Revival" and its anthropological pursuit of collecting fragments of a disappearing Scottish culture and its old-world folk manners — bedtime prayers, hymns, popular tales — produced large volumes from English publishers to be enjoyed by an international audience.

It should not be surprising that Arnold's analysis of an organic Scottish culture appeared at the same moment that imaginative and political understandings of Scottish nationality began to reveal the fracturing contradictory tensions of industrialization, modernity, and the globalized arrangements of the nation's cultural presence. Celtic Revival folklorist Alexander Carmichael headed into the northern Highlands and Western Isles to record Gaelic oral histories and daily customs of the pre-modern crofter during the same historical period that the lowland industrial capital of 1885, Glasgow, was called the "Scottish Chicago" for its sprawling urban concrete and steel expanse, underground railways, hydraulic electrical power, sewage systems, overcrowded steel factories, and booming leisure industry for its middle-class beneficiaries.[4] And in this same decade, while a Free Kirk minister, James Barrie, was penning his quaint moral "Kailyard" or "kitchen-garden" tales about the happy village of Thrums for a large American and English readership, Scotland's citizens were migrating at a rate higher than any other British region, as they had done for decades, to imperial sites in Africa, Asia, and North America to take advantage of military, trade, and investment ventures. Nonetheless, this "earlier reality" of the old Highlands and the agrarian hinterlands served as a central image for forming the national characters of Scotland, Great Britain and North America. Charles Withers explains, "The region has national associations precisely because it has been made in the minds of outsiders and because the historiographical creation of how we have believed the Highlands to be has been both more enduring and more fascinating (and enduring because it has been fascinating) than our knowledge of the changes in Highland life and economy."[5] As both an ideal of capitalist industrial development and an old culture reflecting the folk customs of quiet and remote villages, crofter economies, and timeless local aesthetic expressions, the historical intersection of these two competing versions of Scotland has positioned Scotland ambivalently upon the cutting edge of modernity as well as within the dusty halls of European antiquity. As this book demonstrates, this contradiction continues to hold a sturdy position within Scottish representation. Eleven decades after Carmichael suggested that authentic Scottish culture was an endangered species, a national referendum in 1997 granted Scotland its own parliament with tax levying powers, at the same time that the most internationally recognizable image of Scottish culture, *Braveheart*, an undeniably sappy cinematic spectacle written by an American tourist about the mythic Scottish medieval military hero William Wallace, was being produced and distributed from Hollywood, California, by an Australian expatriate. A case of *Brigadoon* all over again.

However anachronistic, deterritorialized, or incommensurate these juxtaposed examples of Scottish cultural representation may seem, they can too easily mystify the lived material contradictions of gender, class, and racial inequalities within a modern democratic state. That is, most at stake in this discussion is not that Mel Gibson's politically conservative Scotland is any more or less authentic than that proposed by the recently energized "left of center" Scottish National Party, but how each negotiates the terms of national discourse in relation to internationally enforced divisions of social power and oppression. National discourse, according to Homi Bhabha, tends to mystify existing social differences by asserting its own permanence and the reality of its distinctive identity. With a theoretical nod to Jacques Derrida, Bhabha's "double session" of nation suggests that the nation's claim to its own "self-presence" reveals an impossible relationship between a rootedness in an unchanging organic identity *and also* in new forms of collective enlightenment and innovation; nations simply cannot be unified by a permanent essence while also being grounded in "new" and multiply developing differences of the social world.[6] In other words, the problem is not that *Braveheart* is false because of its radical distance from historical accounts of the period but because the pursuit of the "true nation" against a false one uncritically reproduces the discourse of authenticity with its own totalizing claims about national identity and selfhood that end up proving no more useful than "will the real Scotland please stand up?" The struggle since the late 19th century to determine the "real" past or present Scotland has enjoyed such prominence in discussions of the nation's culture that the liberatory challenges to obvious state systemic practices of capitalist exploitation, racist imperialism, and patriarchal violence become banished to the fringes of the debate. And despite the irrationality of authenticity, it would be equally foolish to ignore the changing historical determinations that make claims to the "real nation" a persuasive means for either addressing or ignoring material social divisions.

Gendered Homes and National Affect

All this is not to say that the nation is not real, but that in Scotland, according to such studies as Murray Pittock's *The Invention of Scotland* and Withers's *Gaelic Scotland*, national identity has been so frequently manufactured through narratives of its heroic Gaelic and Celtic pasts, that these fictions have gained a formidable, and quite real, stronghold in the public imagination. This book therefore connects the lived reality of these representations of nation to a much larger modern cultural expression of what I call a *national home*. By national home, I mean a space that is at once emotional and physical, delineated by fixed material local boundaries like the household, the neighborhood, or national frontier, but also imbued with equally impermeable feelings of safety, unity, comfort, and familiarity. National homes recall our earliest memories of the collective self wherein social identities are formed and preserved both by their seemingly permanent access to the self's origins and the ongoing maintenance of their limits — or by what they are *not*. They are all at once what we used to be, what we are, and what we should be. National homes link the boundaries of place, identity, and tradition to the economic, racial, and gendered practices that form the "home-life" of the modern nation-state.

Although national homes often appear uncompromisingly fixed in the case of Scotland, they are as much a social construction or invention as Freed's *Brigadoon*. Since the nineteenth century, the prevailing version of the Scottish national home has taken the form of a middle-class domesticated space as the point of origin from which national identity, private property, and economy seem organically to emerge. The "inside" of the enclosed private dwelling is overwritten with the virtues of the "outside" state and "public" marketplace; thrift, duty, discipline, productivity, and efficiency are emphasized in a highly disciplined local economy. Economic forces of industry appear to be natural extensions of home practices. Rather conveniently, the national home offers an idealized permanent and self-generating sanctuary exempt from the realities of work, profit, and gender or racial subordination. In other words, the national home's ideal is at once timeless and in full accord with modern capitalist life; it presents itself as the organic blueprint of contemporary social order and cultural practice.

While mythic narratives and images are nothing new to national discourse, national homes go further by regulating appropriate collective *feelings* of nation by appealing to emotions that are purportedly both shared and accessible to every individual. Affect affirms the sovereignty of the nation by invoking memories of betrayal, heroism, and justice to bring certain people and values together through highly charged sensations of pride, grief, anger, and hope. As Benedict Anderson explains in his highly influential *Imagined Communities*, national sentiment produces "affective bonds," which draw people together through their association with a particular history, culture, or territory. He writes that "it is useful to remind ourselves that nations inspire love, and profoundly self-sacrificing love."[7] However, in national homes, affect functions as an ideological instrument to cloak, ossify, and enforce social inequalities. Feelings are paradoxically presented both as part of one's private life *and* a collective national activity. Differences of race, class, culture, and gender are thus assigned attendant appropriate emotional behaviors that uphold the "natural" harmony of the nation, dictating what, for example, women or migrant worker "tinkers" are *supposed* to feel about the nation in different ways than others.

The social rules of affect enforce modes of relation and the codes of interpersonal exchange between individuals in a community. At times, the economy of affect identifies those who need to be disciplined for acting outside of their assigned roles. Narrative crisis and social transgression in Maclaren's *Beside the Bonnie Brier Bush*, for instance, is marked by the disharmony of women's affect. When a teenage daughter leaves for the city to seek pleasure outside of the domestic sphere, ministers publicly grieve, men cry, and fathers curse, emphasizing the need to bring women's expression back to their proper place in the home. In other instances, affect describes a sense of privileged ethnic belonging, abundantly evident in the discourse of the contemporary international "Scottish Heritage Industry" and its many clan societies, which link one's current identity across time and space to a heroic history. According to Emily Donaldson's book-length study of Scottish games in America, it is the "shaking up [of] the genes," when she hears the pipers and drummers, "sending a chill up the spine and a tear down the cheek."[8] In MacDiarmid's famous 1926 long poem, *A Drunk Man Looks at the Thistle*, the inebriated excess of raucous anger, pride, despair, self-hate, and lust represents an idealization of direct action, masculine desire, and bold national resistance against English cultural dominance. Still further, the much-heralded 1997 Scottish-Parliament referendum included voting campaigns suspicious of nationalism's emotional history outside of legislative affairs, emphasizing instead the hope of a definitively non-affective response: the Tories' "Think Twice" strategy was paralleled by the Scottish National Party's posters of Mel Gibson as William Wallace reading, "Today it's not just 'Bravehearts' who choose Independence — It's also Wise Heads — and they use the ballot box!"

Feminist studies of the historical division between the heart and the mind — between emotions and rationality — clearly illustrate that these categories have served to socially limit, control and dismiss women's expressions. Ann Cvetkovich persuasively argues in *Mixed Feelings: Feminism, Mass Culture, and Victorian Sensationalism* that being "sentimental" or "sensational" in the nineteenth century became a means not only for banishing women from the public sphere, but also for dictating the terms of political and cultural legitimacy. Representations that "exaggerate reality [to] create extreme, and hence, false emotional responses," she explains, are rendered "aesthetically inferior, morally suspect, or politically retrograde."[9] It is not as if men were not emotional, but their discourse was recuperated by the masculinized terms of wrath, grief, righteous compassion, dedication, and so on. Scholars like Nira Yuval-Davis have pointed out that "unity" and "sovereignty" in public discourse have historically attempted to bar women from the relevant political and cultural domain. She explains that "women did not just 'enter' the national arena: they were always there, and central to its constructions," even though these constructions have presented women as barriers to progress, victims of external influence, or disinterested custodians of cultural traditions.[10]

The changes and uncertainties of modern Scottish identity and its self-representation frequently revolve around negotiations of national manhood as means for garnering individual, cultural, and collective power. National belonging and hegemonic masculinity have been profoundly intertwined through state-sponsored, as well as unofficial images of military prowess, colonial expansion, sexual potency, paternal rule, and civic heroism.[11] As Anne McClintock has argued, national identity is always gendered and functions as a central structure of male selfhood, especially as it responds to the shifting tides of modernity: "[T]he needs of the nation [are] typically identified with the frustrations and aspirations of men."[12] The traditional image of men as individually sovereign and impenetrable wholes moves in lockstep with representations of the nation as a unified cultural and physical territory maintained by unambiguous frontiers of culture, space, and transcendent power. Much of the discussion of Scottish identity necessarily runs into an analysis of masculinity and its struggle for social authority against the increased influence of women in public society and the persistent history of cultural marginalization. For Scottish identity in the last century, the affective economy of the national home has thus served the interests of hegemonic masculinity quite efficiently in repeatedly asserting an ideal Scottish-clad free-moving male subject who lives economically and socially beyond, as well as within, the narrow confines of the local culture and its women. From the London-educated first-person narrators of James Barrie's bucolic Kailyard fiction (1890s), to the home-grown Highland hero in Neil Gunn's *Highland River* (1937), to *Braveheart*'s Wallace, Scotland's local life colorfully nurtures the national male subject who goes on to acquire broader literacies and skills of a more modernized, more independently masculine, and ultimately, less Scottish society. Even amidst the valuable popular critiques of industrial society presented in Lewis Grassic Gibbon's 1930s trilogy, *A Scots Quair*, and Danny Boyle's cinematic translation of Irvine Welsh's *Trainspotting*, the greatest moments of hope appear when their working-class heroes transcend the provincial flaws of their overly "domestic" immediate communities. This modern version of the famous "Lad o' Pairts" myth reflects the paradox of contemporary subjectivity, which celebrates an imaginative return to "roots," "culture," and "ethnic origins" as it also dictates a departure from them towards progress, change, and individual growth. Yet the struggle for male autonomy is by no means static because, like culture, the practices and interests of the plural forms of masculinity, as R.W. Connell has explained, "are inherently historical; and their making and remaking is a political process affecting the balance of interests in society and the direction of social change."[13] These narratives and images of return and departure are presented as national feeling and cultural belonging, but serve in shifting ways a series of persuasive, but often unacknowledged, justifications for male privilege.

Scotland's Home

The Scottish national home provides a particularly compelling case of modern identity formation because, despite not having statehood, Scotland's position as a nation has remained largely unquestioned. Since the 1707 Act of Union with England and Wales, Scotland's identity as a nation has been maintained through expressions of ethnic, linguistic, and religious distinctions, generally described as Scottish culture. Much has been written about the fact that after Union the national institutions of the church, schools, and legal system have remained largely unchanged and particularly "Scottish." That is, key components of civil society, those institutions that lie between the citizen and the state, were able to develop independently of England, despite the cultural and political dominance of English society. The crown and parliament governed and legislated public law, but in Scotland much of local social development remained distinct. After the Union, the Presbyterian Kirk regulated education, morality, health, and death; Scottish aristocrats, like the Duke of Argyll in the eighteenth century, sustained their system of patronage with little interference from London (in contrast to the strict control asserted on leaders in Ireland); Scottish economic enterprises were relatively free of English regulation; and locally appointed managers proposed and enforced local law with almost complete autonomy.[14]

Scotland, therefore, never fully assimilated into the British state primarily because it held on to enough its own institutional structures that would continue to nourish a sense of difference through its independent political, economic, and cultural identity. This element of Scotland's history has fueled national identity and nationalist movements, and ironically, has served as the rationale for British Unionists to reject further cultural or political separateness. In all cases, however, what is never questioned is that a Scottish nation exists, a claim that contemporary populations in stateless collectivities such as Quebec, Puerto Rico, and Kurdistan have found harder to make. From the 1707 Union to today's nascent Scottish Parliament, the struggle in Scotland has revolved around how the interests of the nation are to be defined, preserved, and developed. As an "imagined community," to use Benedict Anderson's term, the Scottish nation is a community that shares values, history, cultural practices, traditions, and territory. It is imagined, not because it is unreal, but because nations depend on an unrelenting fiction of wholeness and unity, to maintain a "self" that is at once different from other nations and sovereign in its own identity. After all, nations do not ever propose their own dissolution, regardless of the political or military conflicts within them.

In this last century, much of Scotland's most explicit expressions of national sentiment have taken the form of energetic cultural and political nationalisms. The assertions of Scotland's distinctive identity can be traced back several centuries in the nation's history, but it was not until the founding of the 1886 Scottish Home Rule Association that official organizations effectively formed in the hope of reshaping the terms of nation laid out in the Act of Union. The eighteenth and nineteenth centuries in Scotland were marked by a few scattered agitations, rebellions, and protests against national injustices even though the ruling elites of Scotland were mainly Scots resting comfortably within the privileges Union afforded them. Despite the popular support of some insurgent movements, however, after the 1745 Jacobite Rebellion resistance relied little on nationalist icons or expressions of Scotland's *cultural* independence to make its case, since most of grievances were not directed at the English but at those who had much to gain from maintaining allegiances with London. This is not to say that there were not any images of Scotland's cultural distinctiveness, but that such images were not commonly employed by oppositional movements. By the end of the eighteenth century, the working-class "people's poetry" of Robert Burns and the anthems of the Jacobins, for example, could be — and were — celebrated publicly for their Scottish character because, for the most part, they had become politically harmless to Scottish and English landowners.[15] James Macpherson's fraudulent 1760 "discovery" of a medieval Highland poet named Ossian, and later the novels of Sir Walter Scott, romanticized Highland life and its clan system, exoticizing its members as primitively passionate, melodic, at times even heroic, but ultimately as too provincial to be aligned with modern modes of political and cultural progress.

Many studies of Scotland's cultural distinction in the last century have focused on Scotland's organized nationalist movements and their energetic response to the region's marginal economic and cultural status within the British state. The sites that I examine in the subsequent chapters demonstrate an interest in the less organized discourses of national identity rather than with official nationalist party politics. Some the most complex and vibrant expressions of national culture are located in such popular sites as Hollywood film, literature, and the recent growth of international Scottish Clan Societies, as well as what occurs in the Scottish National Party. Official nationalist parties have contributed to the discussion in important ways, especially in keeping the status of nationhood and statehood constantly in question with ongoing public challenges for home rule, devolution, and independence, but nationalist parties have never dictated the terms of these debates. For instance, while the SNP has always held an explicitly nationalist agenda, those outside the party and its legislative or electoral forums also speak in the name of Scotland's interests, successes, and failures. Alice Brown et. al. have addressed this point in suggesting that the Scottish Labour Party and the Scottish Liberal Party are in many ways as "nationalist" as the SNP.[16] According to a 1997 British election survey, over 50 percent of Scots say they are either "Scottish and not British" or "Scottish more than British," numbers which far exceed the highest support numbers the SNP has ever received.[17] Such sentiments, which acknowledge Scotland's cultural, even ethnic, distinction, are reflected also in the most official sites of "high culture," as it is in Edwin Muir's 1941 poem, "Scotland 1941": "We were a tribe, a family, a people.... / Courage beyond the point and obdurate pride / Made us a nation, robbed us of a nation." Despite the fact that Muir repeatedly distanced himself, and his work, from organized nationalist politics, his lines invoke images of loss and feelings of collective national unity.

The repeated references to legislative and party politics here and throughout the text are indications of my awareness that cultural analyses of national identity are related to material social effects evident in political arenas and states as well as in everyday practices. In some sites, this awareness involves an agenda made obvious in the texts themselves. For instance, the interwar "Scottish Renaissance," which I explore in Chapter Three, describes a modernist literary avant-garde, which included the prominent voices of Hugh MacDiarmid, Neil Gunn, and Lewis Grassic Gibbon, who deliberately offered their poetry, fiction, and cultural criticism to social resistance and representative politics, not just aesthetics. Their polemical approach sidestepped what Raymond Williams has called the contemporary "true crisis in cultural theory" of the conflict "between [the] work of art as object and the alternative view of art as a practice."[18] The walls historically separating culture and state politics, imaginative writing as art and imaginative writing as social practice, were torn down as national unity was conceived as inextricably linked to the strength of the nation's cultural products. And this tradition has continued in such places as Alasdair Gray's internationally acclaimed fiction, wherein the motto "Work as if you lived in the days of a better nation" prominently appears at the outset of several of the novelist's works. More often than not, however, the desire for self-determination, cultural renewal, or just plain economic fairness has resembled the comment made by the famous Scottish folk singer, Dick Gaughan, in 1978: "Although I couldn't really be called a nationalist, like all Scots I'm very aware of the fact that Scotland has had a separate history and culture [from that of England]."[19] Frequently, as in the example of Gaughan, "I'm not a nationalist, but...." declarations are followed by an acknowledgment of a lived legacy of injustice. Gaughan explains his recording of the revolutionary Jacobite anthem, "Such a Parcel o' Rogues in a Nation," as a bitter ingredient in the composition of Scottish life: "In the wake of the abortive Jacobite risings, the government came up with a 'final solution' type of policy calculated to deal with Scots for ever [sic], by using the politics of greed. That it worked is all to [sic] obvious."[20]

In the last one hundred years, Scotland's official and unofficial nationalisms have vibrantly identified the fact that Scotland is in the peculiar position of being a nation, but one that does not enjoy all the material privileges of self-definition that statehood provides. Scotland is much more than a region; it is an identifiable culture that has faced its share of hegemonic discrimination and assimilationist forces that have devalued and marginalized Scottish identity in Britain: T.S. Eliot echoed Arnold's Victorian attitudes in 1937 by asserting that Scottish culture was a "lower grade" participant and mere "satellite" to English writing, while more recently British Secretary Ian Lang stated to a Scottish Liberal MP in 1992: "You chaps gave Ireland home rule in 1886, and look what happened!"[21] The view that Scotland not only should not govern itself, but *could* not govern itself, appears in concert with the sense that Scottish culture had its heyday at one time, and may be useful as a peripheral curiosity from time to time, but for the most part has since become exhausted of its cultural vitality. Anyone who lives in or knows anything about Scotland can see beyond the absurdity of these claims. More precisely, the nation's marginality reveals how Britain has historically constituted itself by drawing cultural and material resources away from Scotland towards interests located in England and its imperium. When Scottish journalist George Rosie asked an English civil servant in 1995 why British governments had been so reluctant to give Scots home rule, the official candidly gave him the list:

> One, oil. Two, gas. Three, fish. Four, water. Five, land. The oil and gas are self-explanatory, even now. Fish might not mean much to the British but it is a superb bargaining counter in Europe. Water will be important one day, I suspect. And as for all this [gesturing to the Scottish hills] well, this is our, how shall I say it, breathing space. That bit of elbow room that every country should have.[22]

that, in terms of "development," Scotland and England have followed roughly the same general pattern of economic prosperity. Scotland may not have economic parity with England, but the nation has, on the whole, materially benefited from Britain's industrial and global policies.[32] Put another way, Scotland has indeed been underdeveloped by England, but British imperialism created thousands of opportunities for middle-class Scots as military officers, clerks, administrators, and entrepreneurs at home and abroad. As Theodore Allen has illustrated, even just across the Irish Sea, Scots had long prospered as landlords, constables, and bankers. Scots were "junior partners," Allen explains, in the control of Ireland.[33]

I therefore find it important to measure carefully the terms of Scottish nationality against the postcolonial nationalisms in African and Asia that have, at times, fought for cultural and political self-definition in ways that sound strikingly similar what one might hear in Glasgow or Edinburgh. Ashcroft, Griffiths, and Tiffin have maintained that the decolonizing needs of non-white postcolonial nations should not be transposed onto the struggle against English hegemony evident in Scotland, Ireland, and Wales: "...while it is possible to argue that these societies were the first victims of English expansion, their subsequent complicity with the British imperial enterprise makes it difficult for colonized people outside Britain to accept their identity as post-colonial." Ghanaian writer Ama Ata Aidoo links the assumption of a generalized political kinship between Scotland and her homeland as an assimilationist, if not menacing, move in her 1977 novel, *Our Sister Killjoy*:

> One [Scot] had said, "You say you come for Ghaanna? Then we have a lot in common!" Sissie didn't know what to do with the statement, uncertain of whether it was a threat or a promise.
> "We had chiefs like you," the Scot went on, "who fought one another and all, while the Invader marched in." Sissie thanked her, but also felt strongly that their kinship had better end right there.

> > Livingstone the Saint
> > Opening
> > Africa up for
> > Rape.
> > Scottish missions everywhere
> > In Tumu-Tumu and Mompong–
> > > They did love the familiar
> > > Mountain air, those
> > Hardy Highlanders![34]

The increased interest by scholars and students in postcolonial voices and the theory that has come from them should thus make us more, not less, attentive to the particular histories that prevent the view that Scotland's position in Britain is somehow "postcolonial," or that its resistance against the "Invader" is conceptually interchangeable with decolonization movements in Africa and Asia. At the same time, the fact that ordinary Scots participated in the administration of Empire does not forbid the analytical tools offered by postcolonial theory to explain the antagonisms, contradictions, and social differences apparent in the representative national projects that speak on behalf of Scotland. Rather, it should push us further to investigate the specific conditions of struggle and the complex processes of differentiation present in such contested categories as "Scottish culture" or "Scottish people."

Where *Is* Scotland?

To return to Tinseltown's unsuccessful search for its authentic Scottish village, the case of *Brigadoon*, a story ironically centered around the disappearing magical Highland paradise, demonstrates how narratives about cultural identity are mediated by memories, both invented and real, of landscape and the social traditions associated with them. It also illustrates that images of place and people are often produced "elsewhere," perhaps increasingly so as technological media have accelerated the means by which these images are created and distributed to a more spatially diverse and dispersed group of consumers. The fact that Scotland was not Scottish enough for what would be, in the end, a largely American viewing audience underscores how national identities travel across time and space to be interpreted and defined by cultural and corporate entities with enormous influence over how representations are translated, packaged, and made available to the public.

What the makers of *Brigadoon* found most important was that Scottish culture adorn and enable a commodity — not that the commodity enable or adorn Scottish culture. The film was clearly invested in speaking *about* Scots in a particular way — thick accents, kilts, bagpipes, plaid and the like — but was not interested in speaking *to*, *with*, or *for* Scots. As such, it offered an American fantasy of Scottish culture processed and simplified to fit the film-musical package of song, magic, dance, and romance, which ultimately should tell us more about the desires of American viewers and the affective and economic relationships they have with the narratives, images, and characters of popular film. In looking at this example, it is perhaps easy to dismiss the Scotland of *Brigadoon* as a crude appropriation of a national culture, a caricatured manipulation, if not downright erasure, of truth. Yet, we should be cautious of clumsy "us" and "them" propositions, particularly because these same images and symbols — national kitsch — can be found in Scotland, owned in Scottish homes, produced by Scottish industries, and distributed by Scots. One does not have to look hard to find evidence of the "commodity nationalism," to use Anne McClintock's term, of military tattoos, Saltire flags, plaids, trinkets and whiskey.[35] These transportable icons on the one hand articulate a desire to maintain a connection with a lost or fractured community as symbols of pride and memories of belonging. On the other, kitsch items illustrate the modes of meaning-making in capitalist society wherein human relationships are measured, understood, and maintained through the exchange of goods and services. The Rabbie Burns figurine that reads "Made in China" under its boots, a Scottish Lion T-shirt sewn in Mexico, or the *Scottish Life* magazine written and printed in the United States, all demonstrate how the commodity symbols of national life at once represent a cultural expression of national identity and the international productive economic forces that generate and stabilize their presence in everyday life.

The Scottish Heritage Industry, as I discuss in Chapter Four, has been instrumental in transforming Scotland's largest and most profitable industry from manufacturing to tourism. Supported by Highland games, clan clubs, holidays and Scottish societies as well as over three decades of public investment from what McCrone has called "the central nervous system" of Scotland's tourism, the Scottish Office, national kitsch, and the mythic images that sustain it, as well as the American, Canadian and English dollars that largely consume it, are now considered essential to the fiscal well-being, in terms of employment and commerce, of the nation. It is therefore impossible to treat Scottish heritage as a nationally discreet phenomenon for no other reason than that Scots now economically depend on the international proliferation of a *Brigadoon* version of Scottish society. Answering the question "where is Scotland?" thus depends on an awareness that, like any representation, what is "Scottish" can exist not only in many different temporal and territorial sites at once, but that its meanings will change according to the locality and the organic histories found therein. Indeed, even the most commoditized symbols of Scottish history are socially contested, and thus do not exclusively "belong" to the Scottish heritage industry or the meaning-making systems that bolster it. The battlefield at Bannockburn, where Robert the Bruce defeated the English army in the fourteenth century, for example, serves as a pilgrimage site for museum-goers interested in conservative Scottish heritage versions of heroist history, but it is also the starting point for the Scottish National Party's annual "march to independence" in the name of "home rule" initiatives. These contradictions are not solely the provenance of the texts themselves. After all, we are only talking about a grassy field. At stake are the ways in which cultural identity and national histories are attached to this plot of land and how these interpretations are used to promote very real changes in everyday life, not only to those living in Scotland, but to the international tourists impressed by the nation's home-spun legend of David-ly courage against a Goliath-sized alien oppressor. Popular forms of Scottish culture are not simply the result of political mystification, nostalgia, or consumer passivity, but their images, historical narratives, and traditions provide a means for understanding trends in self-expression and the changing modes of cultural production. The increased international interest in "heritage" is not particular to things Scottish, but rather one of the latest ways in contemporary liberal discourse to name a sense of attachment to cultural, ethnic, or biogenetic attachments. Heritage speaks of inherited traditions enlivened by "cultural" activities and the display of old-world folk practices. Not exactly culture and not exactly history, heritage describes a privately experienced affective link to past communities mediated both by bloodlines and a consumer relationship to the symbolic artifacts of a previous society. In other words, in heritage we see the particularly postmodern construction of difference and identity as individually administered and self-fashioned, imagining itself separate from contemporary local practical human relationships. "Finding one's roots" through genealogical studies, stories of patriarchal family traditions, or participating in cultural festivals may seem harmless in themselves, but in practice they propose an exclusivist version of cultural subjectivity that can disregard the historical realities of power and privilege that have made, and continue to make, these identities possible in everyday life. For instance, despite the Confederate flag's legacy in America as a symbol of state-sponsored racist terror in the United States, proponents for its public display by government institutions have asserted its beneficent role in preserving "Southern Heritage." If a formulation of the American south (and all of America) as (white) heritage can abstract its identity from the history of slavery, Jim Crow legislation, and economically enforced poverty, it can will away feelings of (white) shame and replace them with (white) pride. On the other hand, there is a clear difference in assertions of heritage amongst populations of color and historically marginalized communities to resist homogenizing forms of assimilationist identities. "Plantation Heritage Tours," for instance, have become popular amongst middle-class African Americans who visit sites in the South where family members and others endured the brutal conditions of chattel slavery. Yet, even this practice remains consistent with the logic of history as a consumer spectacle available to those who can afford it and presenting historical communities in isolation to present conditions of property, work and education. Simply put, never far behind heritage's celebrations of bloodlines, cultural greatness, and family roots are the processes of racial, class, and ethnic identity formation under the laws of liberal discourse wherein social difference and culture are a "choice."

While there are many forms of Scottish heritage, its industry and public presence suggests that Scottish culture and its history have an unusually wide appeal, especially amongst white Americans. Over three hundred clan societies exist in the United States alone, dozens of Scottish festivals and clan gatherings are held annually by "Scottish Americans," as they call themselves, whose families haven't lived in Scotland for generations. The United States Congress even declared each April 4 as "National Tartan Day" to acknowledge the nation's Scottish heritage activity. The fact that Scottish culture, or some version of it, exists in North America cannot be argued. What is harder to explain is why. Philosopher Charles Taylor has written that with the development of modern identities, individuals are conceived not only as distinct, but as having "inner depths" that can be expressed through a relationship with "originality" and communities that foster the image of this distinction:

> Just the notion of individual difference is, of course, nothing new.... What is new is that this really makes a difference to how we're called on to live. The differences are not just unimportant variations within the same basic human nature.... Rather, they entail that each one of us has an original path which we ought to tread; they lay the obligation on each of us to live up to our originality.... Expressive individuation has become one of the cornerstones of modern culture.[36]

For white Americans who at some point or another have discovered or been granted some relation to Scottish ancestry, their "expressive individuation" has projected itself as a community with its own distinctive culture and identity.

As the recently published *How the Scots Invented the Modern World: The True Story of How Western Europe's Poorest Nation Created Our World and Everything in It* illustrates, efforts to distinguish Scottish culture and its influence too easily become navel-gazing braggadocio within the conservative histories of "great men" and individual geniuses whose "inner depths" of culture most likely propelled them to tremendous power, fame, and wealth. This narrative of civilization by Arthur Herman, the director of the Smithsonian's "Western Heritage" program, demonstrates that what is so attractive about Scottish culture, amongst the many heritage identities that white Americans could claim ancestry to, is that first, Scotland's legacy as a distinctive and unthreatening social space provides a comfortable imaginative home for middle-class whites to articulate their own cultural difference. Second, in an age where communities of color and women have worked hard to have their particular cultural practices recognized, this "inner depth" of Scottish heritage conveniently functions to legitimate white male identities and the privileges socially ascribed to them. Indeed, according to Herman, virtually all of what we know to be modern civilization can be attributed in some way or another to the greatness of Scottish men:

> As the first modern nation and culture, the Scots have by and large made the world a better place. They taught the world that true liberty requires a sense of personal obligation as well as individual rights. They showed how modern life can be spiritually as well as materially fulfilling. They showed how a respect for science and technology can combine with a love for the arts; how private affluence can enhance a sense of civic responsibility; how political and economic democracy can flourish side by side; and how a confidence in the future depends on a reverence for the past.[37]

Like other myopic and unsubstantiated histories of its ilk, such as *The Mark of the Scot: Their Astonishing Contributions to History, Science, Democracy, Literature and the Arts*, Herman's primary argument is that *his* culture did it better, while the other cultures, on their own accord, because of their own moral, spiritual, social, and intellectual faults, failed. Even moments in Scottish history that have been deemed acts of injustice or abuses of power by virtually every historian, British colonialism in Asia for instance, are recovered as good works: "For all its faults and shortcomings and hypocrisies, this liberal imperialism did manage to transform India into a more humane, orderly and modern society."[38] Put another way, the economic and racial advantages that white Britons and Americans of Scottish descent have enjoyed for centuries in the United States and elsewhere, according to Herman's right-wing history, are deserved completely. Such racist fantasies of heroic bloodlines reflect the dominant rhetoric of liberal pluralist multiculturalism, which abstracts identity from historical realities of oppression and masks how these realities are still experienced by currently marginalized populations.

The various cultural sites that imagine Scottish history and national identity illustrate the changing ways Scotland has been both haunted and substantiated by the ghost of the bonnie Highlander and "auld Scotland." The cultural function of this nostalgia is thus not only to reveal contemporary fantasies about social life in Britain and North America, but to address the changing modes of defining the self in relation to historical and present communities. Further, the Scottish national home illustrates a contradictory response to modernity's emphasis on autonomous and free-moving individuals, at once dislodging identity from historical, national, and transnational realities of assimilation, subordination, and privilege, while also constructing an affective connection to a community that shares a history and a set of cultural practices. Together, they problematically propose a cultural subject who is at once connected and disconnected, a depoliticized identity that can privately celebrate the "best" of a culture while ignoring subordinating social divisions and struggles for solidarity against institutional power that are deeply embedded in its public practices.

Chapter Two

THE HOMELY
KAILYARD NATION

In his broad survey, *Modern Scottish Literature*, Alan Bold warns against quick dismissals of the popular late nineteenth-century "Kailyard School" of fiction: "[W]e should be wary of categorizing the kailyarders as sentimental fools; they were men who had a shrewd judgment for public taste and the public responded by adoring the intellectually undemanding entertainment the kailyarders produced."[1] Bold's evaluation of the Kailyard (literally, cabbage patch) and its unavoidable presence in Scottish literary and cultural history illustrates the tension between "public taste" and high art, between "entertainment" and serious intellect, that still gathers around these national tales. The Kailyard's national and international appeal has primarily been explained, as Bold has above, by a tautology that depends on a self-evident and static public taste, which has very little to do with history or culture. We are told, in other words, that the Kailyard was popular because it reflected popular and, we are to assume, vulgar tastes. The cantankerous modernist Scots poet, Hugh MacDiarmid, certainly had this in mind when in his 1926 poem, *A Drunk Man Looks at the Thistle*, he mourned this "preposterous presbyterian breed" of popular fiction which had tossed "real" Scottish artists "owre the kailyard-wa."[2] Bold echoes this argument at another moment in describing the less lofty Scottish verse of the 1920s as "a homemade product cultivated in the kailyard and handled by amateurs."[3] Not surprisingly, George Blake's 1951 book-length study of the Kailyard School, the first of its kind, also follows this pattern in condemning the prose as a "mass of sludge,"[4] told by a "small fry" caste of bard who strolled "through the heather with a claymore at his belt, or ... lingered round the bonnie brier bush, telling sweet, amusing little stories of bucolic intrigue as seen through the windows of the Presbyterian manse."[5]

The Kailyard's mass audience forced those wanting to defend high cultural standards into an uncomfortable position because an impressive number of middle-class readers demonstrated more interest in the morally affirmative and conservative sensibilities of these national tales than in "high" art and aesthetic criteria.[6] Characterized by its simple versions of pastoral Scotland rather than the thematic seriousness of historical representation, Kailyard fiction arranges its exotic scenes of caricatured backwards folk figures around interchangeable conventional tropes and themes of love, covenantry, and sentimentalized rural life to contribute to a mythic depiction of Scottish history. Its authors were journalists and Kirk ministers rather than officially trained artists, and their stories appeared in the Rev. W. Robertson Nicoll's religious periodical the *British Weekly* (subtitled *A Journal of Social and Christian Progress*) and William Howie Wylie's *Christian Leader* rather than in high culture literary journals.

It was no secret that Kailyard fiction stood outside the walls of acclaimed literature, but this did not prevent its authors from enjoying prolific success. Ian Maclaren's *Beside the Bonnie Brier Bush* (1894), for example, drew such a wide readership, including Queen Victoria and W.E. Gladstone, that by 1908 it had sold 256,000 copies in Great Britain and 485,000 in the U.S.A.[7] In his subsequent American book tour, Maclaren fulfilled 96 reading engagements in 27 days along the eastern seaboard of North America, grossing nearly $36,000 in appearance fees and book sales.[8] The reading public certainly had a hearty appetite for the Kailyard product. The *British Weekly* reported that S.R. Crockett's *The Lilac Sunbonnet* had sold 10,000 copies in the first day of publication and promised the quick printing of a second ("making 18,000").[9] Kailyard novels continued to be bestsellers in Britain throughout the period of 1888 to 1901, and, for a six-year period from 1891 until 1897, Kailyard authors ranked in the top ten annually in the American best-seller lists.[10] Kailyard prose was indeed popular, but it also gained the reputation of representing the *real* Scotland — authentic literature peering into the heart of the Scottish nation, culture and life.

In this chapter I am primarily concerned with the ideological work the Kailyard performs in constructing the Scottish nation. I use Mary Poovey's definition of ideological work which doubly emphasizes that narratives are the "work of ideology" within a system of representations that function in concert to bring meanings, like nation, to individuals. At the same time, representations like the Kailyard contribute to "the work of making ideology" by constructing and contesting specific versions of nation, consolidating a vision of Scotland while also inevitably revealing the contradictions within these images.[11] With this in mind, I want to argue that Kailyard narratives and their widespread readership fit comfortably with end-of-the-century bourgeois anxieties about the excesses of urbanization, overpopulation, and moral "decay," as well as New Woman politics, the liberal municipalization of social programs, and the declining influence of Britannia's coercive imperial military arm. The consumption of Kailyard literature outside of Scotland — in England and even more so in the United States and Canada — suggests that the popularity of these narratives responds to anxieties that extended beyond the realities of Scotland. The vision of an idyllic community appealed to a bourgeois nostalgia for the "stable" land and labor structure of aristocratic patronage and the ease of paternalist country gentry life, parish rule, and the strict control of deviant citizenry in the face of increasing economic disparities between the discontented lower classes and the purported triumphant middle class. In other words, the Kailyard illustrates the nostalgia for a lost condition of a happy national home. The reactionary impulse of the "cabbage patch" fiction mediated contemporary tensions of Western industry by imagining a pure and secure society of cultural harmony.

In the first half of the chapter I argue that no nation is essentially real or magically conjured into existence, but that the justification of its existence and truth must "live" somewhere. Viewing fictions of nation as "home" enables us to see how the naturalized notions of private property, morality and gender are woven together in the Kailyard to become the natural habitat of an ideal image of national prosperity and productivity that hegemonically reinforces the values of the ruling class. The Kailyard maintains the integrity of its "national home" within an imagined space of the Highland, a fiction that only slightly resembles the reality of the region's centuries-old intense political and cultural conflict. I also demonstrate that Kailyard authors were only a part of a larger cultural industry that drew attention to Scotland's Highland and agrarian lowland folk ways as a cultural birthplace of national and international modern traditions. As the second half of the chapter shows, the highly contested history of Scotland's countryside is sidestepped in favor of a culturally coherent affective economy whereby social distinctions of nationality, gender, and race are understood according to an emotional caste system. References to class distinctions are gently circumvented in favor of essentialized differences of feeling. Yet of central concern to the national home is the affective maintenance of gender. The woman of the auld-world hinterland, integral to the emotional balance of the nation, is both revered and dis-

> You could generally tell an Auld Licht in Thrums when you passed him, his dull vacant face wrinkled over a heavy wob. He wore tags of yarn round his trousers beneath the knee, that looked like ostentatious garters, and frequently his jacket of corduroy was put on beneath his waistcoat. If he was too old to carry his load on his back, he wheeled it on a creaking barrow, and when he met a friend they said, "Ay, Jeames" and "Ay, Davit," and then could think of nothing else.[25]

Words like "wob" and "round" bring the language of the narrative voice to a more colloquial speech, but it stands in stark contrast to the representation of the extreme dialect of the caricatured local figures. In speech and manner, the narrator is drawn to be both part of and separate from the community — the assimilated native who translates his "folk" ways into the international marketplace of cultural discovery.

The politics of Kailyard authors were certainly aligned with a national clerical identity of Presbyterianism, which identified itself as distinctly Scottish. After all, the triumvirate were all Free Kirk ministers at one point in their lives before they left their parishes for journalistic and literary careers. However, they also supported a more pluralistic and permissive individualism amenable to capitalist progress. This reformist doctrine ran against well-established Kirk covenants emphasizing, for example, stricter proscriptions for personal (emotional as well as material) humility, accountability to the parish, clerical authority, and distrust of modern social improvements. As members of the Free Kirk, Kailyard authors were part of the tradition of a "liberal" Presbyterianism that was institutionally instantiated in 1843 when over one-third of the 1200 ministers walked out of the General Assembly of the national Kirk. As I argue later, doctrinal distinctions go a long way in defining a home that enjoyed the class privileges of national "progress" without its destructive and divisive effects.

Like Scott's Waverley hero, the Free Kirk narrators inhabit a vantage point authorized by the new fashions of modernity and liberalism, though still connected by blood, birth, or sympathy to folkish ways. In pointing out the exotic idiosyncrasies of the "natives," the narrator becomes the master of their peculiarities, infantilizing their intellect, speech, and customs, while offering a non-threatening, placid picture of country life. S.R. Crockett similarly foregrounded the difference of colloquial dialect from standard English with characteristically lengthy passages of careful phonetic approximations of Scots speech. For the English, Canadian, and American reader of popular fiction, these moments might have been a chore to decipher, as in the following description of the newly appointed village minister:

> Syne he sits doon, decent man, as he had a good richt to do, on the green seat at the endo' the hoose, an' wi' great an surprisin' diligence he reads Scotsman till maybe half-past twal. But he has had cracks forbye in the bye-gaun, wi' a farmer thad had been at the smiddy, wi' John Grier the tea-man, wha is an elder o' his an' never contres him in the sesson, an' forbye has sent twa tramps doon the road wi' a' flee i' their lug, I'm thinkin'.[26]

Crockett anticipated that Scots dialect would be a challenge to his English-speaking readership. His narratives are framed with numerous editor's footnotes of translations and explanations anticipating a bewildered reader. His novel *The Lilac Sunbonnet* (1894) was accompanied by a seven-page, double-columned glossary. Compared to later projects that represented Scottish dialects, however, such as Hugh MacDiarmid's 1920s and '30s synthetic Scots, the increased interest in literature printed in Gaelic, or even the widespread presence of Gaelic in the Highlands and agrarian lowlands at the end of the nineteenth century, the speech of Crockett's text is no radical departure from what could be called standard or mainstream English.[27] Crucial to the Kailyard project was that the English and North American reader feel only marginally alien — and never alienated — from the ways of the Scottish agrarian villager. The translation of a phonetic Scots into a printed form of English creates what Anderson calls a "united field" of vernaculars consolidated to make its readers belong to its community of speakers.[28] The linguistic difference of local speech supports, rather than undermines, a fictional sense of nostalgic continuity between the Scottish village and the international metropole.

Nevertheless, Crockett's, Barrie's, and Maclaren's sketches were received as legitimate representations of Scottish life. Of Crockett's the *Stickit Minister, The Glasgow Mail* lauded, "No one acquainted with Scottish rural life will fail to recognize the truthfulness of these humorous presentations, alike as regards the mental attitude and mode of expression common among our Scottish peasantry."[29] Another contemporary reviewer wrote that Barrie's *Margaret Ogilvy* was "setting before us the most beautiful description of a little Scots village household ever drawn, a picture which every line is ideal yet every touch absolutely true."[30] The middle-class reader's own position as the outsider peering at the attractive museum piece is legitimized upon entering the Kailyard community. The mawkish construction of the village in the narratives thus projects the ideal of the private bourgeois home onto an entire community as a protected, unadulterated "domestic" space, which builds the identity of a nation upon a history of a harmonious Scotland that never existed.

edge of critique aimed at the still strong anti–Celtic sentiment in Britain. Carmichael a bit too conveniently turns the table to attack English behavior, relying on national distinctions that ignore the fact that urban Scots were also practitioners of prejudice against those from the Highlands, Isles, agrarian low-lands, and Ireland. Nevertheless, the brief acknowledgment that folk tradi-tions are dying because people have been struggling to maintain a way of life at odds with British modernity indicates an interest not merely based on aes-thetic admiration, but also political sympathy. Attributing the disappearance of Gaelic oral literature to "Reformation, the Risings, the evictions, the Dis-ruption, the schools, and the spirit of the age," Carmichael traces three cen-turies of Scottish history in a sentence to conclude:

> The risings harried and harassed the people, while the evictions impoverished, dispirited, and scattered them all over the world. Ignorant school-teaching and clerical narrowness have been painfully detrimental to the expressive language, wholesome literature, manly sports, and interesting amusements of the Highland people. Innumerable examples occur [*CG* 24].

Above all, the tragedy seems to be the loss of the language, arts, and cultural activities. Interestingly, the populist Jacobite risings of the mid-eighteenth cen-tury against the English crown are lumped together with compulsory English-language schooling and the religious zeal that apparently interfered with the peaceful agrarian life. It seems that the best thing for the Highlanders of the "auld" ways would have been if *nothing* had happened because in no way could their lives have been any better. Again, this suggests a longing for bliss-ful period when all political conflicts of class, culture, and gender were non-existent and resistance was unnecessary.

The sympathy for the Scottish folk in the Celtic Revival is not quite for the community itself and the political process of creatively reshaping its ways amidst social transformations, nor is it for the hardship that Scottish farmers endured in the face of these changes. The implicit hostility towards the lower classes of Scotland and Britain not part of the Gaelic Highland, evidenced in Carmichael's swipe at the English working poor, reproduces a conservatism that impatiently rails against the vulgarity of the mass in the name of national character, while simultaneously identifying with a romanticized and rapidly dying mythic folk home of national expressions and middle-class cultural val-ues. The moment culture is abstracted from the people that produced it, and the history that it is attached to, it becomes a commodity neutralized of its political content, then reinstantiated as a transcendent form potentially avail-able everywhere as either a leisure accessory or an artifact of study.

A New Morality: Tradition, Progress and Profit

W. Robertson Nicoll has been credited for being the marketing expert behind the Kailyard success. He published many of Barrie's and Maclaren's early sketches, and became an advocate of Crockett's work by printing much of it in his journal, *British Weekly,* which first appeared in 1886. He was both praised and criticized for his keen sense of popular interests and the huge publishing profits he gained from them: "[A]t an early age he made up his mind that the object in reading a good book and the only object in reading a bad one is to convert them into hard cash."[52] As Whigham Price has explained in his study of the prolific editor, Nicoll saw two groups merging as the audience for his journal: the well-read churchgoing liberal stratum who belonged to literary societies and stood evangelically against the English; and the recently established middle-class populace of bankers, merchants, and housewives who were eager to acquire literary cultural capital:

> He kept them informed about politics and church matters, telling them what they ought to think; and he supplied them with suitable reading-matter and chitchat which aimed at avoiding the thinness of narrow evangelicism, on the one hand, and the more godless aspects of the world of letters, on the other. There would be nothing that might bring a blush to a maiden cheek; on the other hand, Papa could, at times, be pleasantly titillated, in a highly moral way, to the great benefit of the paper's circulation.[53]

Price's account is better than most in attributing these historical social concerns to class-specific interests. Indeed, the Kailyard responded to an ethos that appealed to the turn-of-the-century professional. But he offers little explanation of why representations of Scotland and its past achieved such prominence amongst an international readership. Kailyard narratives are described *only* as a response — inspired by the authors and editors — rather than a reproduction of contested ideologies that became a part of the practical consciousness of its readership. In other words, Nicoll, the Kailyarders and their eager audience, I argue, not only reacted to culture, they helped make it.

It is at this intersection of a popular international middle-class sensibility and the increased interest in Celtic folk culture that representations of Scotland's mythic past become a national "home" in Highland narratives. Yet, the Kailyard "home" should be seen not only as serving the purpose of mystifying social realities, but ideologically working to perpetuate an image of the home as historically and naturally preceding the contemporary values of industry and profit. The home must be situated outside of the machines of capitalism, while it must simultaneously rest fully in line with them. Kailyard fiction sidesteps this contradiction by appealing to a moral economy that structures and disciplines the behavior of its characters in ways that are never in conflict with the ideals of the profit economy. In fact, in many ways, religion and personal salvation are closely linked to the acquisition of personal property.

Beside the Bonnie Brier Bush provides a compelling example of the overlap of capital and salvation at the moment when the mother Marget employs the biblical story of the chaff and wheat to console a young Kirk minister who has just performed an unsatisfactory sermon. Yet, in Marget's version of the allegory, the separation of the grain from the flax is likened to the process of a mill: "'Ye mean,' said the minister, 'that my study is the threshing mill, and that some of the chaff has got into the pulpit'" (*BBB* 72). The mediation of spiritual purity by the supplemented "threshing mill" rewrites the biblical story to rest comfortably within the contemporary context of machine-efficiency and heightened productivity. While threshing machines themselves were not nineteenth-century industrial technology (they were introduced in 1775), mill machines in all forms were commonly viewed as emblems of industrial society.[54] For Maclaren, one wonders if the inclusion of this mill in the allegory somehow saves more souls in less time. Godliness and commerce parallel each other as values of salvation and profit. The vision of the Kailyard home, like all private spaces, can only justify its separation from the public by supporting the "outside" social mechanisms that make private property possible.

Nowhere is this contradictory construction of "progressive tradition" and "public home" more apparent than in the Kailyard's refiguring of the Scottish church, the nation's moral center. The assiduously recurring themes of moral conversion and catechism go beyond a generically defined brand of puritanism. The moral economy in Kailyard literature relies on the double position of being part of a traditionally Scottish institution while also supporting a historically transcendent "free-subject" ideology of individually defined cultural and financial mobility. Salvation is seen less as a church and community event and more as a personally achieved endeavor that would suffer under the pressure of institutional surveillance, liturgical order or intense public scrutiny. In reproducing this ideology, Crockett, Barrie, and Maclaren repeatedly position their narratives as attacks against an outdated and stultifying creedism of the old Scottish church that opposed the "Wee Frees." In Barrie's story "The Auld Licht Kirk," the narrator, who no longer attends church, stands in stark contrast to the Auld Licht villagers of Thrums and their "Auld Kirk." With almost patronizing reverence, the Auld Lichts are associated with almost comical conventions: "For forty years they have been dying out, but their cold, stiff pews still echo the Psalms of David, and the Auld Licht kirk will remain open so long as it has one member and one minister" (*ALI* 46). While there is an acknowledgment that other churches exist in Thrums, the narrative focuses on the exaggerated zeal in the Established Kirk and the severe demagoguery of their church's ministers:

> So long as the pulpit trappings of the kirk at Thrums lasted he could be seen, once he was fairly under weigh with his sermon, but dimly in a cloud of dust. He introduced headaches. In a grand transport of enthusiasm he once flung his arms over the pulpit and caught Lang Tammas on the forehead. Leaning forward, with his chest on the cushions, he would pommel the Evil One with both hands, and then, whirling round to the left, shake his fist at Bell Whammond's neckerchief. With a sudden jump he would fix Pete Todd's youngest boy catching flies at the left window. Stiffening unexpectedly, he would leap three times in the air, and then gather himself in a corner for a fearsome spring [*ALI* 59].

So extreme is the ranting of the Auld Kirk minister in another moment that the long description concludes with a woman in a nearby pew permanently deafened by the sheer volume of the clergyman's pounding fist. The hyperbolized evangelism is equally attributed to the congregation who, according to Barrie's sketches, fervently watch each other in search of lurking heresy. The Free Kirk, on the other hand, exists in a passing mention rather than an explicitly displayed alternative. Yet, the Established church is drawn with such crude strokes of ridicule that any other ecclesiastical framework would be preferable. Conveniently, the narrator's own "Wee Free" position is not described, except as a private affair properly outside of the constraints of the old Kirk's rigidity.

For Crockett, a more didactic and solemn distancing of the old Kirk is central to an obvious political critique against what are seen as antiquated doctrines. The Free Kirk ideology is represented by meek, compassionate, often younger, emotionally reserved, and personally flawed ministers who are alienated from the church or their parishioners because of narrow local ideals of what a church leader should be. The twenty-two-year-old Hugh Hamilton, for example, who "was placed in the little kirk of the Cowdenknowes," is endowed with nearly angelic qualities but errs in his ability to follow the proprieties of secular social convention. It is obvious where the sympathies of the narrator lie as meek Hugh Hamilton becomes a kind of Christ of the kail with his Highland child-disciples: "There were a dozen of them ever about his knees, listening rapt while he told them the simple stories which pleased them best, or as he sang to them in a voice like a heavenly flute or a lonely bird singing in the first of Spring" (*TSM* 19). His constant hymn-humming, sermons that bring him "high communion with the unseen," and his forgiving temper are contrasted with the impatient and petty natives who trust the fiery patriarchal hand of fear and punishment: "[H]ow is he to fricht them when he comes to catechize them if he makes so free wi' them the noo.... it stan's to reason that there maun be a hantle o' balderdash!" (*TSM* 20). The more sensitive and ultimately compassionate hero becomes a kind of maternal pied piper of the heather who spreads the word of the covenant to the bairns.

At stake for Crockett is the task of producing sympathy for the intellectualism of the minister's faith, fostered by an elite university education, which masculinizes the hero with its rigorous demands of long hours and mental fortitude. But in doing so, the denunciation of the common mass sensibility becomes a critique of the lower class and its backwards attitudes that oppose a cerebral form of worship. Crockett drives home a high/low culture split to energize a valorization of specific class values. Hugh's sermons are unable to "move" the crowd but elevate him to "the sight of the seventh heavens." He is held in suspicion by the village, but is revered in the narrative for his intensely personal (rather than communal) devotion to his faith, and is held in contempt for his asocial wandering despite his rare skill in transmitting meager yet powerful moral words to the "new" souls around him. His position as an educated professional is inextricably linked to a higher order morality, a contrast to the "old" Highlanders' crude desires for a community dictated by authoritarian rule and the dread of eternal damnation. To the dismay of the parish and to the delight of the narrator, Hugh is motivated by his plaintive quest for clarity and salvation, not by the rules of the church. His authority is derived from his proximity to the higher orders of God, nature, reason, and a progressive Kirk. Even though Hugh is "like Him whom he took to be his Master in all things, he longed to lay down his life for the people" and is "too humble to expect his God would so honor him," he is eventually cast out of Cowdenknowes for the fatal flaw of not returning a bow to the wife of "the richest merchant in the place" (*TSM* 20). Underscoring the moralism of the tale, the humble Hugh is buried at his own expense in a forgotten grave as martyr for progressive religious rationality.

The Kailyard hero follows the logic of the Western "free individual," contemptuous of strong community institutions, women, and the "common" tastes of the poorer classes. The unjust codes of social propriety, although attached to the merchant's wealth, are then attributed to the gendered meddlings of the only woman in the tale, the merchant's wife, and then paralleled with the old Kirk's stranglehold on Hugh's search for salvation. Crockett's critique renders the village town a public sphere that is just too public. It is monovocally lethargic, intrusive to soulful worship, opposed to organic innocence, and finally complicit with imposing the historically "private" excesses of irrational feminine whimsy upon the path to progress. Also apparent in this construction is the fact that the citizens of Cowdenknowes are not exactly divided against each other, but are rather set at a distance from the true natural spirit of the nation. This maneuver holds in place a sense of public purity, while still advocating the need for social reform at the individual level. At fault are the morally myopic and meddlesome individuals, not the village itself. After all, the children, as holders of the nation's future, give promise to the new ideology. Crockett's narrative ideologically supports the image of a reasonable Highland tradition renewed by a privately administered connection to history, morality, and nation — those ideals that purportedly transcend the narrowness of the poor and female individuals in Scottish villages who are, nevertheless, found in their midst.

In order to maintain the national character of the religious doctrine, however, the Kirk is revered as an essential element of Scottish culture that institutionally connects the present to the nation's history. In other words, the progress of England is not the alternative to the Auld Kirk. For Crockett this translates into distinguishing a masculine and unified popular Presbyterianism from the influence of both the Anglican Church and, to a lesser extent, Catholicism — presented as threatening Scotland with their seductively colonizing creeds. The tale "Why David Oliphant Remained A Presbyterian" begins with a quote from an English clergyman at Oxford University: "Now, Mr. Oliphant, can you conceive any reason except national prejudice, to which I am sure you are superior, why you should not be with us in the Church?" Reiterating that one of the most valuable resources of the Scottish nation is its male intelligentsia, David keeps the home of the Kail proudly Scottish, uncontaminated by English people even though young Scots are repeatedly tempted by ideals of Englishness. Crockett's story fittingly ends with the main character forcefully declaring, as if he were stating his military allegiance, "with the steady voice and eye that had come to him from his grandfather" that "I must cleave to my own church and my own people!" The fact that the "church" and the "people" become nationally aligned in this instance demonstrates the quick elision of differences within the nation — the very differences that, for example, send poor Hugh to his death or inspire Crockett's Free Kirk polemics.

More importantly, class differences are collapsed to construct a totalized populace unblemished by aristocratic snobbery and "nancy" English values at odds with the nature of the Scottish land and its people. The critiques of the national church are deeply invested in identification with an emergent class of Scottish professionals including doctors, teachers, ministers, and entrepreneurs. As Barrie's narrator explains, "It is surprising that an English church was ever suffered to be built in such a place [Thrums]; though probably the country gentry had something to do with it. They traveled about too much to be good men" (*ALI* 16). In other words, the English Church is *too* private, too full of false social aspirations (although what a true aspiration might be is left unsaid), too personal, and too home-*less* to be counted as a legitimate orthodoxy. As such, it is disconnected from the local public, a synthetic set of cultural sensibilities grafted onto an unwilling citizenry. Where a critique of Anglicanism occurs in Kailyard texts, however, it walks a fine line — not always consistently maintained — to not reproduce what would otherwise be an "Auld Kirk" argument against the Free Scottish church. This line depends on the strategy of masculinizing Scottish characteristics once again into a totalized, univocal, politically sovereign whole against an effeminate, insipid English elitism that crudely demeans every aspect of Kirk tradition. Take, for example, the narrative commentary about the minister who has just returned to "Glen Kells" from an English university:

> There he learned that Presbyterianism had no claims on any man's admiration —
> that Presbytery was singularly unbeautiful — that the Beautiful alone was the
> Good — that a Creed was a most inconvenient encumbrance — that enthusiasm
> made a man hot and ridiculous, whilst the cultured calms and ordered forms of the
> Anglican church, as understood by her higher clergy, were the only things really
> worthy of admiration though even these must be carefully denuded of all meaning
> [*TSM* 151].

The English argument against the Scottish church privileges a passionless and patronizing out-of-touch doctrine, which the narrative suggests would be unable to reach the spirit of the enthusiastic Scottish parishioner.

Still, the "calm culture" that describes Anglicanism in this case could easily be assessed to the liberal spirit of Hugh Hamilton, as could his unconventional solitary bookishness. For Crockett, therefore, simply denouncing the aloofness of the English is not enough to support a critique of the Anglicanism *and* sustain his reformist individualism. His strategy of appropriating the "popular" manly voice of the people in order to show the organicity of Presbyterianism extends to an association of the English church with Catholicism. What the Scots villagers of Glen Kells notice most about the English minister are his vestments of "gown and cassock" and other "vain gauds of adornment" which are denounced by the people as a "rag of Rome" and "nocht less than the mark of the beast." This is more than the oft-rehearsed Calvinist criticism of the Anglican Church's "Purple Papacy." In a move of ethnic distinction pervasive in national discourses, the Kailyard is measured against Catholicism and its fastest growing "alien" manifestation in Scotland at the end of the century: the Irish.

Given the conspicuous absence of the Irish in the Kailyard, this is a particularly telling moment. Since the national home is, of course, an ethnically uncontested space, according to these narratives anyway, the Irish, despite their large numbers in Scotland at the time, had to be all but written out of the picture. Yet as historians and sociologists have thoroughly documented, Irish laborers in Scotland, mostly poor and unskilled, were indeed present and endured severe discrimination and hostility, especially in the industrial centers.[55] The boundaries of the nation are elaborately erected against England's religion, not necessarily as ideologically separate from Scotland's, since, for the Kailyard, there is much that they have in common. It is Anglicanism's inherent complicity with the apparently monstrous face of Catholicism and its Irish agents that are the threat to the unspoken common voice of the Scottish populace. In this way, the Kailyard authors can support their professional positions of being inside the nation, but being untethered by the "backwards" tendencies of the people they purportedly belong to. At the same time, they stand outside the nation as the objective, fully mobile and nonparochial voices who can, and indeed should, speak for the need of new social models available to the national home.

In contrast to the elite liberal male citizen — moral, educated, prosperous, free-thinking and free-moving — constructions of nation like the Kailyard narratives depend on a fiction of gender that inevitably positions women at once inside and outside the structure of the home. However, unlike the double location of the narrator, whose identity is predicated upon the psychological and physical movement between the nation and the modern ideals that may exist outside of it, women's identity is exclusively tied to a version of the home that they neither own nor have agency in defining. Women thus function as the naturalized tenders of the hearth, maintaining the production suggest that women's bodies are ever completely separated from women's labor in social constructions of gender. Flora Cambell is indeed expected to be in the home because she is presented as a "natural" woman. Yet there is no vicarious sense of male sexual pleasure there, or any indication of sexual power; in fact she is completely de-sexed. In distinction from Flora McIvor, she is not the exceptional heroine who is a threat because she uses her individual power. She is in fact drawn broadly as the good woman and potential threat only because she may surrender her power to perform her national duty to home and family. What is important, then, is not only that she be *in* the home (like Flora McIvor eventually becomes), but that she demonstrate her ability to maintain and reproduce the entire domestic sphere and its economy of affect. She is completely overwritten by the Highland community's dependence on her ability to fulfill, from the home, her natural emotional obligation to her father, her minister, her neighbor, and, in fact, the entire social body. The new national flower is revered for ability to keep the social fabric of Scotland's cabbage patch tended and growing.

Nations depend on discourses of affect to construct and inspire a sense of unity and commonality while simultaneously naturalizing the social divisions that make nations possible. Kailyard narratives, in like form, erase differences as they erect them, authoring myths of racial and cultural distinction while reinforcing divisions of inequality and histories of subordination. It is important, thus, to see emotions as a constructed regulatory home wherein the historical tensions between fictions of nation and the feelings of home that appeal to "natural" formations of gender, race, and class are mediated and masked. The popularity of the Kailyard school and the Celtic revival no doubt parallels, reflects, and perpetuates the ideals of the turn-of-the-century growth of the industrial complex and middle-class ideology. In this way we might view the images of the national home in the late nineteenth century as perhaps one of the most efficient ways to sell the message of capitalism.

Chapter Three

MASCULINIZING THE KAILYARD
The Scottish Renaissance and the New Nation

Scotland is unique among European nations in its failure to develop a nation-alist sentiment strong enough to be a vital factor in its affairs.... The reason probably lies in the fact that no comprehensive-enough agency has emerged; and the commonsense of our people has rejected one-sided expedients incapable of addressing the organic complexity of our national life. For it must be recognized that the absence of nationalism is, paradoxically, a form of Scottish-self-determination, which ... has reduced Scottish arts and affairs to a lamentable past to be induced to take different forms and express itself in a diametrically opposite direction to that which it has taken for the past two hundred and twenty years, the persuading programme must embody considerations of superior power to those which have so long ensured the opposite process.
— Hugh MacDiarmid, *Albyn, or Scotland and the Future* [1927]

Edwin Muir's 1938 critical tract *Scott and Scotland* sets out to identify and remedy the difficulties of Scottish identity and authorship. Subtitled "The Predicament of the Scottish Author," Muir's text speaks to the problems of asserting the legitimacy of Scottish nationhood, character, and cultural dis-tinctiveness during the first several decades of the twentieth century. The "predicament" for Muir, who was himself a Scot and a poet of reputation, involves proving the worth of Scottish traditions and its products of "genius" to the world at large — a predicament for sure, given the ascendant interna-tional modernist climate of aesthetic evaluation that railed against anything that could be dismissed for being too culturally specific, too nationally nar-row, or more accurately, too "provincial." At a time when commerce, war, and technological communication drew national boundaries ever closer to one another, provincial described any expression that appeared to be trapped in its own conceptual neighborhood, in sensibilities that could not appeal to the "broader" standards of universality and objectivity that characterized

with English sensibilities but also cloaked Scottish difference in the construction of a unified British state culture. The Scottish Renaissance imagined a more radical break, at times treating Britishness as a tool of English assimilation and cultural denial. The effort of MacDiarmid and others to assert difference in writing by drawing attention to a distinctive Scottish, rather than British, literary identity is what Henry Louis Gates Jr. has described as the necessary process of "self-identification," wherein a people's writings are recognized within a locatable history as constitutive elements of collective tradition and cultural meaning.[12]

MacDiarmid, however, was not so interested in self-identification as an archival project — initially anyway — as the advertisement of his 1922 *Scottish Chapbook* read, "Not Traditions — Precedents."[13] The Renaissance enterprise, instead, lauded itself as a national conversion toward a new consciousness rather than a project of recovery, although methods of recovery were evident nevertheless. Reacting against any evidence of complicity with Englishness and the discourses these authors thought contributed to the devaluation of Scottish culture, the revival took form as a national avant-garde, instituting literary means for a violent break with the past. As was the fashion for so many of the avant-garde writers in Europe, MacDiarmid's 1922 *Scottish Chapbook* begins with a manifesto, "The Chapbook Programme":

> The Principal aims and objects of the *Scottish Chapbook* are:
>
> To report, support, and stimulate, in particular, the activities of the Franco-Scottish, Scottish-Italian, and kindred Associations; the campaign of the Vernacular Circle of the London Burns Club for the revival of the Doric; the movement towards a Scots National Theatre; and the "Northern Numbers" movement of Scottish poetry.
>
> To encourage and publish the work of contemporary Scottish poets and dramatists, whether in English, Gaelic, or Braid Scots.
>
> To insist upon truer evaluations of the work of Scottish writers than are usually given in the present over–Anglicized condition of British literary journalism, and, in criticism, elucidate, apply, and develop the distinctively Scottish range of values.
>
> To bring Scottish Literature into closer touch with current European tendencies in technique and ideation.
>
> To cultivate "the lovely virtue."
>
> And generally, to "meddle wi' the Thistle" and pick the figs.[14]

The "call" for artistic action shares the dramatic force found in the electric ultimatums of the Italian Futurists or French surrealists. It is perhaps telling that next to nothing has been done to place MacDiarmid or his Scottish contemporaries alongside the likes of Tristan Tzara, Andre Breton, or Bertolt Brecht, a few of the more heralded names of the pre–World War II international, "historical" avant-garde, as Peter Burger has attempted to define it.[15] Such an investigation, while beyond the scope of my analysis, would help place the nationalist ideology that was so much part of the Scottish Renaissance into the broader context of art and politics in Europe, not in order to prove that Scottish authors should be granted membership to this group of elite avant-garde authors, as they are often treated, but to show the historical and political continuities that extend into Scotland. Questions of a renaissance in Scotland have rarely gone beyond the discussion of British cultural politics and social relationships.

Ironically, this is what MacDiarmid's "programme" was trying to avoid in advocating an artistic movement aligned "with current European tendencies in technique and ideation." The curiously vague references to Scottish culture's apparent intimacy with Italy and France, two nations with a long tradition of cultural imperialism on both sides of the equator, and who were, not accidentally for MacDiarmid, ardent rivals to English cultural and colonial supremacy, emphasize Scotland's independent cultural alliances with Europe. At the same time, the call for support for local artists and their "distinctively Scottish range of values" sounds a lot like what we might hear today from the National Endowment for the Arts in the United States or the Scottish Arts Council. What registers for MacDiarmid as contemporary European "technique and ideation" takes the epic form in his 1926 long poem, *A Drunk Man Looks at the Thistle*, which quickly became the Ur-text not only of the Scottish Renaissance, but also of Scottish nationalism.

Barbaric Rationality and Drunken Logic

MacDiarmid's *A Drunk Man* expresses the contradictions of being an English-speaking Scot who is simultaneously Scottish and cosmopolitan, progressive and traditional, committed to "culture" but only high culture, and nationalist while proposing an internationalist political and artistic scope. MacDiarmid himself picked up and expounded on the phrase George Smith coined in 1919, "Caledonian Anti-Syzygy," to specifically describe some of the paradoxes in his own work, and critics of MacDiarmid's poetry and the Scottish Renaissance have been equally eager to use this term to explain the conceptual ambivalences in his poetry. MacDiarmid's poetics of Scottish identity were highly informed by the tradition that divided the norms of English civility from Celtic barbarity, but this made it difficult to embrace what had been

gories to generate its watery vision. Solid and sure amidst the linguistic and conceptual indeterminacy of the poem's Scottishness are assumptions about Europe's cultural ascendancy and traditional gender binaries that offer very little room for the nation's common "folk" or women to move.

The "internationalism" of the poem — that is, the frequent references to figures and forms that are not Scottish or English — should be viewed more precisely as a Europeanism along the lines of MacDiarmid's *Northern Numbers* programme: "To bring Scottish Literature into closer touch with current European tendencies in technique and ideation." The link between the Scottish Renaissance and the European arts played great importance in explaining the goals of the aesthetic "resurgence":

> [N]o revival of Scottish literature can be of consequence to a literary aspirant worthy of his salt unless it is so aligned with contemporary tendencies in European thought and expression that it has with it the possibility of eventually carrying Scottish work once more into the mainstream of European literature.[30]

In general, gesturing toward traditions and histories beyond the nearest national boundary was certainly nothing out of the ordinary, as the highly praised work of Joyce, Pound and Eliot demonstrates. In *A Drunk Man*, the fragments of Scottish culture are conspicuously integrated with repeated direct addresses to Dostoevsky, several whole uncited stanzas written by Russian poet Alexander Blok, and lines translated into Scots from the work of Russian poet Zinaida Hippius, Belgian poet Georges Ramaekers, German poet Else Lasker-Shuller, the French Edmond and Rocher Mallarmé, and the American Herman Melville, as well as the mention of the intellectual virtue in the works of Spengler and Nietzsche. Within these references are the invocations of Dostoevsky's terms "vse-chlovek," for a nationless pan-humanity, and "narodbogonesets," meaning a powerful God-bearing collective folk people of an idealized union of all humankind. Likening himself to Ulysses, who travels "owre continents unkent / And wine-dark oceans wander" (34), the narrator turns to Russia as a national peer: "My whim (and mair than whim) it pleases / To seek the haund o' Russia as a freen' / In workin oot mankind's great synthesis...." (122).

The fascination with ideals from the European continent in the poem, foremost among them Russia, suggests an affinity of philosophical concerns across nations, proposing an international "cultural vitality" that, by examining folk practices, might engage in furthering the progress of human development. The narrator directly addresses Dostoevsky, identifying him as a peer in the artistic "action" of invigorating his nation with passion and genius:

85

For a' that's Scottish in me,
As a' things Russian in were thee
And I in turn 'ud be an action....
Till my love owre history dwells
As owretone to a peal o' bells [146].

So if Scotland can be compared to Russia, MacDiarmid, or his narrator at least, is like Dostoevsky, and both are involved in the project of enlightening the globe's masses through their attention to local cultures. *A Drunk Man's* focus is therefore as "great," as, perhaps *The Brothers Karamazov's* and Scotland's folk history is as important as Russia's since neither of them is solely attached to "provincial" concerns but legitimated by its contribution to the highest reaches of elite "Culture" as it is interpreted by the leaders in the arts.

The desire to become a more noted part of Europe's cultural center is, on the surface, meant to move Scotland out of international obscurity, but in effect reinforces the discursive tools of empire. Narratives of universal progress, the enlightenment of all cultures, and the primacy of international elite agents in the process all rely on techniques of cultural subordination and the colonization of differing practices. It is an assumption, as Edward Said argues, that Europe's cultural ascendancy — and those that benefit from it — are not founded on practices of global domination. Objective "progress" relies on a version of history that obscures the geographical and political realities that make the advancement of European culture possible.[31] *A Drunk Man* imagines a particular kind of Scottish nation that has proven its ability to participate in the realm of modernized cultures and that leads the rest of the world with its history of elevated national arts and folk practices.

According to the final section of the poem, such legitimation is contingent on how these national practices can be abstracted into the objective worlds of thought, music, and beauty. The final three hundred lines, called "The Great Wheel," rally rhythmically in a near terza rima to illustrate the circularly developing ethereal momentum of universal psychic progress. The all-encompassing cosmic image of the wheel, reminiscent of the music of the spheres, turns through time as its great "Circles o' Infinity" guide the forces of an elevated "Culture" that transcends nation. The goal of humanity, the narrator explains, is understanding the nature of the wheel such that "we may aiblins swing content / Upon the wheel in which we're pent / In adequate enlightenment" (180). Nation and nationality exist as single units within the universal expanse of the wheel's function: "[H]e canna Scotland see wha yet / Canna see the Infinite, / And Scotland and true scale to it" (182). A fully

tural landscape and that provide "a self-definition, for contemporary reasons, which draws on any elements however improbable, that can be made to inhere in a particular land."[38]

Williams's account is fair in not totally condemning *A Scots Quair*'s "improbable" Golden Age ideal for indulging in fantasy or escapism. Instead Williams describes the ideal as a technique for sustaining hope, of mourning, and of enabling a critique of local institutions. This makes sense if we agree that Gibbon's maneuver does in fact act as a palliative for everyone in the way that Williams supposes. Missing in Williams's assessment of the trilogy is an adequate explanation of this national vision as more than just an imaginative retreat or a fantasy that temporarily numbs the pain of class struggle; it is a representation that reinforces other oppressive social divisions. This vision, although set centuries earlier, reproduces the idyllic and oppressive Kailyard image. The dawn of Scotland that Gibbon idealizes and that Williams explains as a social coping tool constructs a fortress of "neutrality" around patriarchal gender distinctions. The original inhabitant of Scotland, for example, is exclusively imagined as male, sustaining what Maria Mies has called the "myth of the man-the-hunter" technique, which genders evolution and history in such a way to position men as the true innovators of civilization and the sole producers of history.[39]

Women are not absent in *A Scots Quair*, but, as with the myth of the man-the-hunter, they are understood as timeless creatures of nature, who fulfill their instinctive roles as mother and wife while the men engage in "change." Even though the narrative perspective is third person, the entire story is told through the eyes of the only three-dimensional female character in any of the novels, Chris Guthrie, whose most intimate personal trials mirror the social conflicts that affect the community around her, when, for example, the miscarriage of her baby occurs at the same time as the suppression of the General Strike. Even more apparent is the fact the spiritual connection to the "improbable past" is enacted almost exclusively through Chris Guthrie and her quasi-magical attachment to the vestiges of antiquarian Scotland — an element of the novels that exists beyond the scope of Williams' theory.

Throughout, Chris acts as an emotional and social conduit to the nation's early days, who earnestly transfers the energies and truths of primitive culture into the narrative present. The novels are hardly subtle on this point as Chris, in moments of crisis, returns to the ancient druid rocks, or "Standing Stones," as a personal sanctuary:

> Cobwebbed and waiting they stood, she went and leant her cheek against the meikle one, the monster that stood and seemed to peer over the water and blue distances that went up to the Grampians.... [It was] the only place where ever she could come and stand back a little from the clamor of the days [*SS* 106].

These monoliths represent more than just a quiet place for the main character to contemplate; they are the memorials of the dawn of Scotland which, recalling Thomas Hardy's Tess at Stonehenge, provide the novel with moments of existential perspective and truth when sensuously initiated by a woman's touch:

> And then a queer thought came to her there in the drooked fields, that nothing endured at all, nothing but the land she passed across, tossed and turned and perpetually changed below the hands of the crofter folk since the oldest of them had set the Standing Stones by the loch of Blawearie and climbed there on their holy days and saw their terraced crops ride brave in the wind and sun. Sea and sky and the folk who wrote and fought and were learned, teaching and saying and praying, they lasted but as a breath, a mist of fog in the hills, but the land was forever, it moved and changed below you, but was forever, you were close to it and it to you, not at a bleak remove it held you and hurted you [*SS* 117–18].

As the antennae of the nation, Chris's own thoughts become the generic and universal "you," strangely fusing all thought into a collective Scottish mind. It is as if Chris has become the voice of the country, proclaiming its own eternal power above and beyond the temporary human conflicts of the time. The social problems that motivate so much of the text's plot appear in these passages to be less important than the magnetic spiritual pull that grips the land's inhabitants — a reminder that the one relationship impervious to transformation is one's rootedness in nation.

The ties to nation, however, have become more available to Chris than any other character. Her ability to perceive the ineffable force that "held you and hurted you" describes a physical engagement of the body, an emotional connection, not grounded in principles of rationality, that enacts the furtive revelation of nation's truth. Also apparent is the fact that Chris's talent is associated with her femininity: her exuberant sexuality, affective sensitivity, motherly selflessness, and utter absence from the brutal public battles that color the lives of the male characters. Nation and gender overlap throughout the novels, such as when her husband cries, "Oh Chris Caledonia, I've married a nation!" (*CH* 145) or the local Provost admits to have "felt like he was stared at by Scotland herself" (*CH* 110). Through three marriages, three pregnancies, and three homes, Chris, like the land itself, maintains an ageless beauty, as noticed by her son: "I thought just now you looked like a girl. There are some at school who look older than you" (*CH* 172). Her beauty is constantly sexualized by the men folk who talk of bedding her: "Ay, God, she looked a bonny lass still, a bit over-small for her height, you would say, but a fine leg and hip, a warm bit quean" (*GG* 72). At times she sustains an almost romantic relationship with her son Ewan, who she describes "naked, a long, nice naked leg and that narrow waist that you envied in men, lovely folk men, he was standing stretching stark" (*GG* 40). Even women in the novels find themselves attracted to her: "[S]he looked bonny with that dour, sweet, sulky face, the great plaits of her hair wound round her head, rusty and dark and changing to gold. Else thought, If I were a man myself I'd maybe be worse than the minister is — I'd want to cuddle her every damn minute!" (*CH* 75). The magnetic pull from the land that "holds" and "hurts" is transferred onto Chris's body and character as the womanly nation: the mother, lover, and permanent tie to the untainted origins of Scottish life.

The humanist class critique of Gibbon's text inverts the *Communist Manifesto*'s promise of the end of history by imagining a classless era in Scotland that existed *before* history ever began. It also posits Scottish identity as a relationship with the natural properties of the motherland which extends to the heart of each of its "children." Like humanism's construction of an essentially beneficent self or prehistorical, pure social order, Chris's identification with the nation's men (rather than women) of the past privileges male public "social" life over the female private "national" life. On the one hand, the moment that Chris recognizes her connection to the folk that have preceded her is a politically progressive moment of counteracting narratives of individualism. Through her the narrative shows the relationship of present life to the experiences and activities of past generations and acknowledges the ways they have been instrumental in shaping her as part of a cultural collectivity. However, on the other, Chris is never given the agency in the novel to share this information with the "masses" the way her three husbands and son are able to do in rallying the workers against landlords and factory owners. Instead, these moments appear in the narrative as quiet personal reflections that structure the plot's social drama of men.

The other side of Chris's insight into the true nation's reality is the ardently conservative aspect of Gibbon's humanism. The nation described through Chris's reflections is timeless and permanent, a perspective that undergirds the representation of working conditions and labor struggle. Such a framework imagines nation as a pure "core" reality covered over by newer cultural forms of class division, property dispute and the dissolution of communities. What looks like existential perspective in the novel supports an authentic and ahistorical model of a moribund "pure" Scotland corrupted by contemporary social excesses. The effects of this change are nearly insignificant because, in the long run, the land and its mystical presence in the people have remained more or less the same. Chris's epiphanies produce a perspective so broad that they almost completely remove themselves from the tensions of the present. The concept of nation slips away from the arena of the social to become solely experienced as a private communion between an individual and the land — between Chris and the primitive hunter man.

The representation of Scotland in *A Scots Quair* is caught in the paradox of nationalism, proposing progressive changes while relying on a fixed backwards gaze into an idealized picture of the nation's essential social and spiritual make-up. Within this image is a longing for egalitarian social relations, communal labor structures, and an attentiveness to local traditions. Indeed, Gibbon's humanism imagines the nation as having more democratic possibilities than most of what comes out of the Scottish Renaissance. Yet quite evident in this gesture is that the national image of auld Scotland is identified as primarily belonging to the domestic realm — women's lives — while social change, historical struggle, and the progress towards recapturing its ethos remain the domain of men. Chris discovers what is already there; her husbands and son create something *new*. Similarly, women become the mouthpiece, the guardians, and the purveyors of nation and spirit in contrast to men, who are understood to be participants in the arena of labor and *class*. Joan Wallach Scott locates a similar division in E.P. Thompson's history of English uprisings *The Making of the English Working Class:*

> Work, in the sense of productive activity, determined class consciousness, whose politics were rationalist; domesticity was outside production, and it compromised or subverted class consciousness often in alliance with (religious) movements whose mode was "expressive." The antitheses were clearly coded as masculine and feminine; class, in other words, was a gendered construction.[40]

In the case of *A Scots Quair*, nation is drawn as the emotional "expressive" religious component Scott mentions. While it does not quite subvert class consciousness in the text, it does rest as the bedrock and the stabilizing foundation of this struggle and, with its image of unchanging permanence, often questions the possibilities of the conflicts; these differences between Gibbon's and Thompson's texts warrant notice. However, in both narratives, Thompson's historical, Gibbon's fictional, the gendering of class requires the feminine backdrop of the irrational domestic, be it nation or religion, from which the masculine public motor of working-class resistance can be seen to advance.

Gibbon's Scotland has become feminine, however. Quite to the contrary, it constructs two "halves" of Scotland that apparently complement each other: the mystical static image of national sovereignty, and a vision of workers' commitment and solidarity that will transform the injustice of class inequities in Scottish life. Ultimately privileged, however, is the latter, masculine future of Scotland, then supported by the feminine, as women are positioned as the figurative and literal keepers of tradition, memory, and nature, existing amidst the changes of national history, but never as its agents. *A Scots Quair* avoids the avant-garde aesthetic individualism of MacDiarmid's poetic in favor of representations of community and collective action, but it relies on some of the same gender binaries that appear in *A Drunk Man*. In both we see how the rewriting of Scottish tradition constructs a division between the domestic feminine aspect of nation and the "universal" realm of nationless philosophy, or international class consciousness, to uphold their visions of Scottish political and cultural progress.

Where the Boys Are

Nostalgia for the primitive Golden Age of Scotland figures equally prominently, but with a more conservative emphasis, in the prose of the journalist and novelist Neil Gunn, who Hugh MacDiarmid called "the only Scottish prose writer of promise ... in relation to the 'vast engulfing sea' of English literature."[41] Whereas the novels of Gibbon focus on the fractured glen community holding on to what is left of the nation's dawn, Gunn concentrates on the individual solitary male Highlander and his communion with the natural elements of the Scottish landscape in an organic pattern of off-the-land living. His hero, like Chris Guthrie, possesses a "private" communion with the national landscape, but it is clear that Gunn's text wants nothing to do with the national political organization to which Chris's visions find connection.

As is the case with his Scottish Renaissance contemporaries, Gunn's *Highland River* (1937) masculinizes the national home by focusing on male intellectual and physical achievement, but unlike *A Scots Quair*, it is not at all concerned with working conditions, class politics, and popular struggles for an egalitarian society. The focus of Gunn's text is the singular and distinctly middle-class subject whose gender, class, and race privileges exist within a nation of rugged terrain of once ample, now increasingly sparse resources that only the attentive hunter, fisher, or worker of the land can harvest and appreciate. Like the Kailyard narratives, there is a fond portrayal of the pre-industrial way of life in Scotland, but it is one that concentrates on the individual male Highlander instead of the specifics of the glen community. In doing so, his text is able to maintain an idyllic vision of the farm and fishing community, but so briefly that the text effectively depopulates the region in shifting attention to the hardy Scot, who regularly leaves the glen village to enter into the masculine world of the rugged and cold landscape of North Scotland. And with stoic industriousness, simple habits, native manners, and agrarian lifestyle, the male Highlander character stands out heroically as the symbol of lost Scottish culture. Infused with the discourses of individualism and survivalism, Gunn's renaissance suggests a middle-class desire to wander back into a mainly empty national "home" of Scotland to rediscover manhood, which is written into the premodern land and customs of the hermetic Highland crofter.

The novel itself is structured as a memory told by an objective third-person narrator who traces a Scottish man's life, beginning with his adventures as a boy before World War I and extending into the 1930s adult present. Much more than in the work of MacDiarmid and Gibbon, *Highland River* is consistent with the likes of Barrie and Maclaren in establishing an edenic quality to the region's farming villages. All that is missing is the presence of the Kirk:

> The little Highland community in which Kenn lived was typical of what might be found anywhere round the northern and western shores of Scotland: the river coming down out of the wooded glen or strath into the little harbor; the sloping croft lands, with their small cultivated fields; the croft houses here and there, with an odd one on a far ridge against the sky; the school, the post office, and the old church, where the houses herded loosely into a township; and inland the moors lifting to blue mountains.
>
> On flat ground by the harbor were the cottages of most of the regular fishermen, but many of the crofters also took part in the fishing seasons, for wealth was unknown amongst them, and poverty had to be outwitted by all the means in their power. Sea-fishing and crofting were the only two occupations of the people and however the rewards of their labor varied from season to season they were never greatly dissimilar over a whole year or over ten years. Thus in the course of centuries there had developed a communal feeling so genuine that the folk themselves never thought about it. They rejoiced and quarreled, loved and fought, on a basis of social equality. Even the big farm was absent and so there were no bothies and farm servants, and none of the children that went to school had a father who thought of someone above him as "the master" [24].[42]

The passage might just as easily be describing the crofting Kailyard communities of Thrums or Drumtochty with their portrayal of the small country town nestled organically into the idyllic country landscape. More striking is the similar emphasis on the solidity of the community, the long-standing condition of inherent social egalitarianism, and the industriousness of the folk. They are not rich, but not poor either. And, while they are hardworking, no one seems to work for anyone else, all property appears to be evenly distributed and, as the text states, there are no farm servants or masters. It is a place where people live on meager means but are happy, where the community is isolated from the modernized world but independent and self-sustaining, and where, above all, fathers are in charge.

This last point is no small one for *Highland River* since the novel pays most of its attention not to the community itself, as one finds in the Kailyard novels, or in Gibbon's *A Scots Quair* for that matter, but on the developing masculinity of the young Kenn as he grows into adulthood. Set primarily in the years shortly before the war, the narrative follows with a Thoreauian fascination the memories of the boyhood adventures — hunting, fishing, and exploring the abundant rivers and paths of the Highlands — of its main character. The novel is thus a memory of two highly interdependent and socially threatened conditions that, if lost, jeopardize the authentic process in which Scotland's boys are raised: the purity of nature in the Highlands and the essentially free lifestyle of the folk.

These two elements are given almost equal credit for rearing and nurturing young Kenn, as he learns as much from the river wildlife as he does from his mother or father; the land and the folk unite as the force of national authority. In both cases, however, emphasis is given to the necessity of emotional and physical hardiness in the Scottish ethos, as in the description of the character of the land:

> Strength was the keynote of this coast, a passionless remorseless strength, unyielding as the rock, tireless as the water; the unheeding rock that a falling body would smash itself to pulp upon; the transparent water that would suffocate an exhausted body in the slow rhythm of its swirl [58].

Violent and unforgiving, the Highland landscape is infused with heroic, almost warrior-like traits that promise only death to the careless interloper. But to Kenn, who attentively observes the scene, it is also a moment of being instructed by the elements, of truth, and of understanding the secrets of human existence: "However strange and haunted one's thoughts, they were never really introverted; but, rather, lifted into some new dimensions of the purely objective, where internal heats and involutions pass out upon, without tainting, the wind and the sea" (58). Making a loose gesture towards the Romantic sublime, the individual's communion with the elements of nature produce moments of awe and terror beyond all rationality that lead to knowledge of life's essences.

The harsh attributes of the land present quite a contrast to the "small cultivated fields" and "little harbor" that so invitingly describe Kenn's charming village. It is here again that we see the dualized Scotland, the split within the very logic of nation and the Scottish Renaissance's masculinist reproduction of it. The quaint glen community takes on the role of the domestic safe haven, only described when Kenn returns to his home. As such the place becomes overwritten with the qualities of home, where Kenn is bandaged, fed, nurtured, and restored after his treks into the depths of nature. Unlike the Scottish landscape, it is without conflict or tension, an uncontested, and therefore permanently static space:

> The heart of all this winter life was the peat fire. From sledging and sliding, from the cold sea, from snaring birds and rabbits, Kenn came back to his home, entered at front or back door, and held the leisurely dance of the flames [77].

As the place where boyhood activity appears to end, where the lessons of life cease and the ease of security settles in, this "domestic" side of the nation is quite obviously the sphere of women, the only context in which female characters are represented in the novel at all. Immediately after the above description of the hearth fire appears Mom, whose full presence completes the picture:

> His mother presided over this central world with completeness. She was a heavy woman, of easy carriage, with a comely face and smoothly-parted dark hair. The graciousness of her manner came out of a wise kindness. Her presence filled all the house, and Kenn accepted her as man accepts the sun or the storm or, perhaps, God, for Kenn had little sins of omission or commission to think about, and he would wonder now and then — with an evasive smile — what his mother might say, or do, when he entered at the door [77].

Depicted as a kind of fertility symbol, or earth mother, endowed with a pleasantly ample body, she is the moral standard whose omnipresence in the home renders her not just as part of the domestic sphere; her "completeness" in this "central" world makes her nothing but the domestic sphere. Further, she is not just any woman, but a Highland woman, whose humble thriftiness complements her abundant femininity: "[S]he was in truth the figure that tended the fire and dispensed life, and must often have created her bounty out of

of an ancient nation. Quite explicitly, the Resolution suggests that the United States was always and continues to be fundamentally Scottish:

> Whereas this resolution commends the more than 200 organizations throughout the United States that honor Scottish heritage, tradition, and culture, representing the hundreds of thousands of Americans of Scottish descent ... these numerous individuals, clans, societies, clubs and fraternal organizations do not let the great contributions of the Scottish people go unnoticed....[2]

The past is drawn into the present along an uninterrupted timeline of influence, as the "contributions" of Scottish descendants affirm the continued and permanently European character of American society. At the same time, American eminence is linked to an essence of "Scottish people," manifest in the bloodlines of Americans and exalted by the greatness of their social and economic accomplishments.

Although the resolution carries no legislative authority in U.S. law, its impact as a symbolic gesture, sanctioned by one of the country's most officially *national* institutions, illustrates the kind of welcoming space Scotland is currently given in very powerful segments of the American imagination. While the population of Scots in North America dates back to the colonial period, this romanticized notion of Scottish identity says little about the history of Scottish migration and transnational ethnodiasporic communities.[3] Instead, the cult of ethnic influence reveals the way in which a well-organized and established group of Scottish descendants in the United States have generated narratives of ethnic pride, proclaiming an ownership of American culture that has purchase in the national imagination. The Senate's stated appreciation for a loosely formulated sense of national influence goes to the heart of contemporary understandings of cultural and ethnic identity that have congealed around claims to "heritage." In the Senate Resolution, Scottishness does not exactly speak of a relationship with a specific present cultural or political body that might be called Scotland but with a set of Scottish individuals (called "Scottish Americans") whose distant affiliation with a pre–American national tradition — through birth, name, or blood quantum — has transported old-world European values into the fabric of American culture. While Scotland as a nation-state is frozen in time right around the early fourteenth century and the Declaration of Arbroath, Scottishness continues to flow throughout American history by the "invaluable contributions made by Scottish Americans that have led to America's preeminence in the fields of science, technology, medicine, government, politics, economics, architecture, literature, media, and visual and performing arts." It is as if the American cultural body inherited a "Scottish gene" in the 18th century, a recessive trait occasionally emerging to express itself in American history. America is granted a thriving history of its own, while Scotland and its descendants are granted "heritage."[4]

The Scottish heritage movement does not quite comprise an "ethnic community," organized to promote the material, representational, or legislative interests of Scottish Americans, nor is it a "diaspora," as Khachig Tölöyan has defined the term, committed in any meaningful way to maintaining translocal cultural or political connections with a homeland.[5] Devoid of any notion of a contemporary existing collectivity in Scotland, Scottish heritage identity links itself instead to a fantasy of early Scottish life, one that is profoundly mediated and enabled by commodities of "auld" Scottish culture, historical reenactments, and the ever-widening commerce of tourism. As I demonstrate later, Scottish heritage may at times employ the ideological tools of ethnicity — an identification, even loosely, with defined historico-cultural practices of dress, family organization, or religion — in declaring itself a "people," but ultimately it is unlike other white ethnic groups, such as Poles or Italians, in the U.S. that maintain their differences in distinction to assimilation and hegemonic culture. Scottish heritage makes no claims to its cultural marginalization; in fact, its discourse consistently proclaims its place at the very center of American social values. At the same time, like transnational communities with a diasporic consciousness, Scottish heritage has found its cultural currency through an impressively organized effort. More than 300 organizations have formed in the United States around a Scottish culture and Scottish American identity. In fact, this is a moderate estimate, given that there are over a hundred and fifty Clan Associations and Societies alone. Add to these Caledonian Clubs, St. Andrew Societies, Burns Clubs, Scottish Games Councils and Associations, Scottish Societies, Heritage Societies, Scottish Genealogical Societies — all with regional offices and local chapters — and it is easy to see that all things Scottish have become both institution and industry. And not only in the United States, but also in Canada, which passed its own version of Tartan Day in 1991, as well as other white settler nations across the globe: Australia, New Zealand, and South Africa.

Scottish heritage and its narratives of history, race, and national pride represent one of the newest ideological strategies for preserving privileged identities. The first section of this chapter examines the emergence of heritage broadly, not only as a relatively new discursive category of identity politics, but also as a consciously strategic tool for furthering interests of global tourism and commerce. The "commodity nationalism" of Scottish heritage in the United States suggests that its ubiquitous presence in Scottish organizations could not have been possible without the heavy public and private investment of Scotland in advertising, museum construction, estate preservation, and festival planning. Scottishness is certainly an American phenomenon, but not exclusively so, and not one that can be explained in national isolation, especially when international markets work hard to create commonalities among elites across national borders. Never far behind heritage's terms of original national identity, ethnic character, clan pride, and cultural greatness, one finds contemporary interpretations of immigration, racial difference, cultural value, and social success, sites where racist logic today is perhaps most openly articulated. The second half of the chapter thus traces the ways that Scottish heritage's reliance on the discourse of family, genealogy and cultural atavism is closely connected to the history and politics of race in their specific national contexts. And, if anything, heritage's parallel presence in the U.K. and U.S., specifically, demonstrates that the techniques of constructing white identities function hand-in-hand with globalism's celebration of only those differences that have been fully integrated into the marketplace.[6]

Heritage: Amusement Park History

As those who have attempted to trace its uses have found, heritage is an elusive but powerful modern concept that lends historical, social, ethnic, and racial differences an air of legitimacy and permanence in sites throughout the western world.[7] Heritage remains an uninterrogated and slippery term, but generally speaks of the commonly inherited ideals, practices, and property transmitted from a readily accessible past and of an essential and timeless cultural identity. In the face of contemporary change, heritage produces "newly" discovered origins to a mythical homeland that make possible a whole host of fantasies about past cultural and political social orders. These fantasies are then transferred to the descendant, an individual or a group, that can live anywhere. For Scottish heritage in particular, it is the process of finding one's "roots" in an agrarian society of pre-industrial yesteryear. Like Chris Guthrie's Standing Stones (Chapter Three) or Barrie's Auld Licht Thrums (Chapter Two), Scottish heritage reproduces a narrative of an uncontaminated, harmonious, geographically limited, and thoroughly nationalized space.

The Scottish heritage industry's narratives of a mythic and heroic past, as well as its thousands of kitsch products — clan crests, swords, family plaids, kilts, etc. — aim to evoke real feelings of belonging, pride and community in recognizing an historical affinity to a group and its cultural practices. Yet heritage stands at a distance from any version of Scottish life evident in or beyond the 17th and 18th centuries, and it hardly acknowledges the presence of a contemporary and developing culture within Scotland. For this reason, I find myself quite often using "Scottishness," as David McCrone, Angela Morris, and Richard Kiely have coined it, in describing expressions of Scottish heritage to underscore its popularity amongst a very specific slice of international society that in many ways has only a limited relationship to past or present life in Scotland.[8] It is clear that heritage is not history, although heritage is indeed informed by history. More precisely, heritage is a sense of history that is not so much interested in social realities as it is in the spectacle of reenactments, performances, and lifelike icons that illustrate the way it purportedly really was. McCrone, Morris, and Kiely have argued that heritage's ultimate goal of authenticity is less the work of professional scholars and books and more of an emphasis "towards history as a form of entertainment, as 'infotainment.'"[9] Experiencing the past through dynamic, visceral displays is more important than historical evidence, while active participation is more important than detailed knowledge. Like the thousands of American Civil War enthusiasts who stage the brutal battles in military dress, "living history" in Scottish heritage constructs a space wherein the actor or observer can tangibly share a version of three-dimensional realism of the past, outside of conventional boundaries of time and place. No longer the domain of ivory tower academics or bookish intellectuals, history is made meaningful and popularized through a personal relationship with a sanitized version of the hardships of earlier social conditions, or what David Lowenthal identifies as celebratory memorialism, which at the expense of historical inquiry is motivated by a desire to inspire group cohesion — national, family, or regional identity — through a devotional connection with a unique and positive past.[10] Mastery of history is gauged by a commitment to an authentic feeling of the past, but a feeling that ultimately experiences war without death, family without patriarchy, and work without class oppression.

What distinguishes Scottish heritage from many of the earlier forms of international Scottish culture, such as Burns Clubs which encouraged Highland dress at their meetings as early as the nineteenth century, is the way in which it is, without exception, more closely than ever connected to international commerce, tourism, and an expansive array of "kitsch" commodity items. Heritage has become the most convincing contemporary logic of nation in overdeveloped "first-world" middle- and elite-class regions — a depoliticized and mostly conservative "commodity nationalism."[11] Like the modern structure of nation, heritage contains a "common sense" which appears as the recurring spectacle of a self-evident sovereign order and shared values of justice, home, identity, family structure, law, religion and history. In the totality of the image — total because it purports to speak for all — identity, values, and history are imagined as a united "expression" of "our" or "the" nation. The essence of heritage in its current form is inseparable from the commodity-logics of marketing; exchangeable forms provide the means for portions of the citizenry to express and display their national selves. National identity is reflected through the consumption of tokens of the nation rather than through political participation, while power relations and social divisions remain more or less intact.

The link between nationality and the commodity-spectacle has been made perhaps most compellingly in Walter Benjamin's "The Work of Art in the Age of Mechanical Reproduction," where the "aestheticization of politics" describes undemocratic national processes of political transformation. National Socialism was in effect enabled by aestheticized "expressions" of nationality available to a mass audience who were simultaneously prevented agency in the nation's governance. While the totems of nation were readily accessible to all, control of the resources of reproducibility became so centralized that the possibility of dissent was drowned out by the unitary images of national culture: "Fascism sees its salvation in giving these masses not their right, but instead a chance to express themselves. The masses have the right to change property relations; Fascism seeks to give them an expression while preserving property."[12] Benjamin echoes Marx's explanation of the commodity as a "mysterious thing" that seems to magically abstract human labor from a product and then is "perceived by us not as the subjective excitation of our optic nerve, but as the objective form of something outside the eye itself."[13] Put simply, citizenship is not determined through an engagement with the processes of political change but by the consumption of an abundant array of national symbols, goods, and cultural activities that pose no threat to the existing social order. Nation becomes possible for everyone as a symbol, while the actual ability to participate in the workings of the nation is available to only a few.[14] In this capitalist logic of the commodity, national politics becomes a style rather than a struggle for justice and representation, as nation is understood as the image that speaks for itself, but never mentions how it got there and what hierarchies are integral to it.

Tom Nairn's elaborate study of nationalism in Britain has referred to the vast presence of kitsch in Scotland and abroad as the "Tartan monster,"

> recognizable by its symbols, slogans, ornaments, banners, war-cries, knick-knacks, music-hall heroes, icons, conventional sayings and sentiments (not a few of them "pithy") which have for so long defended the name of "Scotland" to the world ... in a London pub on International night, or in the crowd at the annual Military Tattoo in front of Edinburgh Castle.[15]

As Nairn comments, the relationship of "tartanry," or the tartan monster, to middle-class international commercial interests goes back to the early nineteenth-century Waverly and Ossian cults that inspired Scotland's image as a tourist park and continues on through the movement of Kailyard fiction to the late twentieth century. And the critics of these "manias" (as they have been called[16]) have been equally vocal, as was MacDiarmid in their blasting:

> This "Highland" cult is amusing, and it is exasperating.... [I]t gives no heed to history, anthropology, or philology. Originating about a century ago, fathered by Sir Walter Scott and Stewart of Garth (mother unknown), it has been fostered ever since by our military and feudal caste, tartan kilt-makers, sellers of souvenirs and advertisers of whiskey.[17]

Several decades later, the ubiquity of contemporary commodity Scottishness usually provokes the same kind of ire that leads Nairn to the following outburst: "How intolerably vulgar! What unbearable, crass, mindless philistinism! One knows that Kitsch is a large constituent of mass popular culture in every land: but this is ridiculous!"[18] Commodity nationalism, and its diasporic, transnational variant, which Nairn calls a formidable "sub-nationalism," has, along with heritage nationalism, continued to appeal to middle-class sensibilities of beneficent country gentry and happy clan folk — but in the contemporary forms of commodity nationalism, Scottishness is regarded as something not only to be seen or observed, but to be owned, as an artifact and as a very part of who you are.

Heritage's complicity with global capitalism's rationalized depthless market of consumable products of culture can appear irreversibly total, as real national differences — not to mention social divisions of power — are erased by mass trinkets that create the spectacle of "Scottish" life. Take, for instance, the American Scottish Coalition's official advertisement for Tartan Day 1999, which reads like an invitation to the Scottish Disney World:

Bring on the pipers, fiddlers, drummers & dancers! Proudly wear the kilt, the sash, your tartan pin and tartan tie. Play a round of golf, the national game. Plan a video party and watch, "The Blood is Strong," "Local Hero," "Tight Little Island," "Culloden," "Rob Roy" or "Braveheart".... Celebrate your heritage by dancing a Scottish country dance, toasting the Haggis, and sipping some Scotch whiskey.[19]

If a national culture can be reduced to the images of leisure activity, cuisine, Hollywood film (*Trainspotting* is conveniently omitted), and costumes, the possibilities for political transformations of nation become limited to consumer choices about mass-marketed artifacts of culture. History is subsumed by heritage while one's identity is measured by the accumulation of goods. The British historian Robert Hewison writes of this cultural phenomenon as the ever-diminishing "real" behind heritage's hyperreal:

> History is gradually being bent into something called Heritage, whose commodity values run from tea towels to the country house. Its focus on an idealized past is entropic, its social values are those of an earlier age of privilege and exploitation that serves to preserve and bring forward into the present. Heritage is gradually effacing history, by substituting an image of the past for its reality.[20]

Not the real, but "the desert of the real itself," as Jean Baudrillard has described the spectacle of contemporary culture, a "simulacra" that, rather than simulating the real, masks, perverts, and eventually replaces all relations to history with references to its own persuasive image of the limitless accumulation of leisure products.[21]

In terms of heritage it is easy to see how the desert of the simulacra extends deep into Scotland in reproducing its culture, not through a process of exploring the dynamic social struggles that are its history, but via a pastiche of consumable objects and nostalgia marketed as emblems of Scottish life. However, to capitulate to the logic of commodity relations and to treat it as having completely and finally co-opted the entirety of culture itself would be a mistake. Regardless of the totalizing rationality of this global "culture industry," as Adorno and Horkheimer have described it, Scottish culture is in fact experienced, both in Scotland and abroad, in ways that "heritage" cannot account for.[22] Fintan O'Toole puts this into perspective in citing a friend who, when hearing people talk about "Scottish culture," recalled the growing molds and bacteria that sickened children in Glasgow's poorly heated public housing. When she heard the phrase Scottish culture, she reached for her fungicide.[23]

In the same way, Jean Baudrillard's famous essay "Precession of the Simulacra" explains Disneyland as a fantasy machine built to make the rest of

America appear authentic and real. But the argument also assumes that every-one, including perhaps the Mexican concession-stand worker in Frontierland, interacts with the spectacle of the Magic Kingdom's hyperreal in the same way the white tourist from Paris might.[24] Culture is consumed and repro-duced from multiple social positions contingent upon race, sexuality, gender, and class in ways that cannot be accounted for by an assumption of culture's complete cooptation by the commodity spectacle. Theorists of heritage thus tend to overstate their point, as does Hewison: "Heritage is a fantasy, the commodification of our past and present means that in the enterprise culture, we surely do know the price of everything, and the value of nothing at all."[25] The simulacra of heritage represents a persuasive element of culture but can-not be so abstracted from the range of contested social differences that it replaces culture altogether. Hewison and others quite accurately recognize that the entertainment business of capitalism thrives on glosses of history that depoliticize social differences and erase their power relations, yet commerce and "enterprise culture" do not necessarily include the scope of relationships that work to resist the totalizing ethos of the marketplace's commodity-driven identities.

Nevertheless, identifying heritage within the Western, and increasingly global, hegemony of profit is indispensable in tracing the economic trail of heritage. In Britain and Scotland, major civic redevelopment initiatives and private commercial enterprises have been strategically promoted as heritage programs. According to sociologists David McCrone, Richard Kiely, and Angela Morris, who have written the only book-length study of Scottish her-itage, *Scotland—The Brand,* "In Scotland, heritage and industry are inextri-cably linked. The Scottish Tourist Board is in many ways the central nervous system of the Scottish heritage industry."[26] The latest international interest in Scotland corresponds with major governmental expenditures aimed at assisting the shift from manufacturing to service occupations. The 1980 British "Heritage Act" was instrumental in accelerating funding to tourism by estab-lishing a £50 million National Heritage Memorial Fund. While avoiding any explanation of what heritage might actually be (Lord Charteris, when asked what the word meant, replied, "Anything you want"[27]), the Act also allowed the transfer of property defined as heritage to the state in lieu of tax and indemnified museums against the cost of insurance.[28]

Museumry was brought forcefully into the marketplace of leisure and tourism as monies poured in through tax incentives and set-up funds to pri-vate heritage sites that, unlike most museums of earlier decades, began charg-

alism of Scottish heritage. Nonetheless, he does finally admit, "Heritage is a reflection of nationalism in its widest sense."[43] For McCrone and others it may seem unsettling to place the largely bourgeois phenomenon of clan societies and kitsch marketeering alongside the vibrant history of nationalist organization that has characterized a significant part of Scottish politics in this century. The fact that heritage and party nationalism still share many of the same tools of national discourse should not be underestimated when we consider that Bannockburn, the site where Robert the Bruce's army defeated the English in 1314, is currently overseen and marketed by the heritage office, National Trust of Scotland, but also has served as a symbol of the SNP since the 1950s in their annual "march to independence." Certainly, their interpretations of the event lead them in vastly different directions. The frequent reference by most clan societies to Bannockburn describes their family's individual participation in the heroism of independence for ancient Scotland; for the SNP it represents a long and ongoing history of collective political definition.

Nairn also recognizes the relationship of heritage, or "tartanry," to nationalism, but he constructs a hierarchy wherein "real" political nationalisms stand over and above the "cultural sub-nationalism" found in pop-culture kitsch-imagery. Wary of explaining nationalism too much by cultural factors, which "can lead to an over-subjective or idealist diagnosis of the country's modern situation," Nairn is nevertheless aware that the broad reach of tartanry "will not wither away, if only because it possesses the force of its own vulgarity — immunity from doubt and higher culture. Whatever form of self-rule Scotland acquires, this is a substantial part of real inheritance bequeathed to it."[44] Granting heritage a formidable place in Scottish culture permits Nairn's study to cautiously approach its implications, astutely concluding that its tradition of sentimentalized savagery smacks of an ultra-patriotic British Unionism. What his analysis refuses to grant, however, is that the low-culture philistinism of this "cultural sub-nationalism" deserves the same attention for its political interests, motivations, and effects as those found in a nationalist party. Heritage is not politics, in Nairn's view, but a crass cultural cretinism that along the way produces its own particular political allegiances. This may be true, but the logic of heritage has found its home in Scottish culture for centuries and thus cannot be dismissed as an aberrant phase of modern identity; rather, it is one that has continued a tradition of resiliently and profitably deflecting claims of its "low culture" to become the international paradigm of Scottish identity.

The Invention of Tartanry

Heritage's romantic past relies on myths and legends to carry its nostalgic vision of essential Scottish culture from the annals of the golden years into the present. The symbols of Scottishness, from clan tartans to images of the rugged highland warrior, refer to "traditions" supposedly embedded in the nation's social origins. Although myths are an important part of heritage, they are not presented as myths but as permanent conditions. The distinction is an important one because to label a narrative of the past as a myth is to question its legitimacy. Traditions, on the other hand, are treated as self-evident, existing independently of interpretation. They are essences of a given reality that are not "told," but experienced. The national identity of heritage takes place in the material process of transforming myths into "legitimately" performed tradition. Specific narratives from and about the distant past are given that Frankensteinian electric charge of "truth," granting the inanimate tissues of the tartan monster a life of its own. And with the spark, the "double session" of national time whereby present reality exists simultaneously with an unchanged past is enacted. In similar ways, Raymond Williams argues that tradition:

> ... has been commonly understood as a relatively inert historicized segment of social structure; tradition as the surviving past.... What we have to see is not just a "tradition," but a selective tradition — an intentionally selective version of a shaping past and pre-shaped present, which is then powerfully operative in the process of social and cultural definition and identification.... What then has to be said about any tradition is that it is in this an aspect of *contemporary* social and cultural organization, in the interest of the dominance of a specific class. It is a version of the past which is intended to connect with and ratify the present. What it offers in practice is a sense of *predisposed continuity*[45] [emphasis in original].

For nation, tradition produces not just a sense of continuity, but also a sense of community, of group cohesion and the social structures that define it. Traditions are invented, but they depend on the institutions of culture to ideologically support them.

Tartanry, including kilt-making, clan plaids, and Highland garb, has proven to be a central component of Scottish heritage, both in its production and its criticism by an intelligentsia distrustful of its populist claims to original cultural tradition. Historically, tartanry provides an interesting case because it was one of the first examples of heritage commodity nationalism, emerging as a popular social phenomenon in the middle of the nineteenth century, just as capitalist commerce in Britain was taking firm hold. More recently, as in the case of Nairn and others, it is a way of describing the gaudy

un–Scottish Scotland), as well as the scores of contemporary books illustrating with detailed appreciation the hundreds of different family patterns, indicate that tartan, regardless of whether it is "real" history or invented myth, remains a lively tradition in Scotland.

Tartan may contain different meanings in different contexts, but it is important to acknowledge that the institutional resources devoted to redefining tartan as a fanciful, "neutral," and thoroughly marketable symbol of Scottish culture have moved and will continue to move alternative interpretations of it farther into the social periphery. The Scottish Tartans Society's goal to "reduce confusion in and the trivialization of tartan" is accompanied by a registry full of tartans ascribed to international private corporations, exclusive social clubs and state territories, which proves that the heritage motive of enterprise is always close at hand: "[The tartan's] global acceptance has produced a marketing emblem that could not be bettered."[57] Scottish styles are good investments, apparently. But just as the demand for tartan has created a market symbol, the marketing of the symbol has produced the demand. In this way, heritage is profoundly connected to the transformation of traditions into commodities, highlighting the most ideologically palatable aspects of tourism, as well as blending history and myth to create an entirely profitable image of nation.

Heritage as Endangered History

Much of the commodity's appeal within heritage nationalism is that products of Scottishness are presented as both timeless and endangered. The language of preservation and conservation is fundamental to creating a need for the immediate consumption of a soon-to-be-extinct tradition that extends to the beginnings of history. This is the contradiction seen in Scottish Tartan Society's aims: to preserve original documented patterns (including those of the Wilson weavers) of the first clan tartans, but also to cultivate an endlessly individuated number of unrepeated plaid styles that, according to one founder, is meant "to encourage generally the wearing of Highland dress."[58] By owning a kitsch item, an individual not only participates in Scottish culture but helps to give it greater life. Take, for instance, a flier I received in my pursuit of the seemingly endless channels of Scottish heritage that offered one square foot (95 dollars' worth) of Scottish land:

> Own a piece of your heritage and preserve a piece of Scotland for perpetuity.
> Have you ever dreamed of owning a piece of your Scottish heritage or consid-

ered preserving a part of the remaining undeveloped beauty spots of the World?[59]

The tiny Highland parcel of "beautiful unspoiled land," overlooking Ullapool, 500 feet above sea level, is presented first as a naturally pure and permanent space that the earliest of Scots might have encountered. Second, the land is endowed with a cultural legacy by being near the "once home of the Author Sir Compton Mackenzie of 'Whiskey Galore' fame." And finally, it is given a proud history: "To the left of the land lies the point where the ship 'Hector' sailed to Pictou Nova Scotia in 1773 loaded with Scottish pioneers." Inviting the consumer to become an owner and a trustee of this triumvirate of nation — nature, culture, and history — the magic of the landscape is then smartly packaged into its distributable heritage form, a Deed of Trust, "registered in the Books of Council and Session in Edinburgh, Scotland. Beautifully presented in a folder with detailed maps, perimeter displays of the horizon, a title deed on vellum, with historic information."

The scheme reproduces the fundraising paradigm in the era of privatization, when individual pledges are solicited to support public projects ranging from stadiums to playgrounds. Important in this case, however, is the way in which this one square foot of land is rhetorically situated within, and sold by, images of national history and personal ("my") heritage. Never explained, or even mentioned, by the flyer are the forces endangering this section of the Highlands. There is an oblique reference to development, as if modernity as a whole is jeopardizing the sanctity of the national landscape, yet there is no indication that the preservation initiative is motivated by any specific environmentalist concerns that would explain, for instance, how the Highlands are littered with nuclear missiles aimed at NATO's latest litany of "rogue" nations. Highlighted instead is that my heritage is something that not only can be owned, but should be owned by me and other Scottish descendants worldwide so that we can partake in some form of Scottish nationality. And while it is not defined, heritage refers to the unstated values nostalgically fixed on a premodern nation, preserved in its contemporary form by private property, acquired "for perpetuity," and the attractive ornament that legitimizes it. The abstract notion of heritage appears as an abundant resource to those who seem to have inherited it through family name or bloodlines, but seems most available to those who can actually possess, and so "preserve," their very own authentic piece of it.

Yet heritage is not just property or the commodity, but the relation of national cultural identity to these artifacts — some mass-produced, some handcrafted — of music, fashion, sport, arts and food. While participation is certainly practiced through the consumption of Scottish cultural goods, heritage is also about the formation of private social groups dedicated to preserving the forms and rituals of Scottishness. With the many Scottish organizations in existence today, the act of *joining* is a central mode of participating within the heritage movement. Without exception, Scottish organizations and clan societies are explicitly invested in a loosely defined preservation project: "to preserve and promote the customs, traditions, and heritage of the Scottish people educating the public as to Scottish history, literature, music poetry [*sic*], art, and architecture."[60] These words, taken from the mission statement of the international Council of Scottish Clans and Associations, appear with slight variations in virtually all Scottish clubs to ensure that their version of what constitutes tradition remains intact.

Private social organizations of Scottish culture in themselves are not a new phenomenon: Burns Clubs, literary groups now officially numbering over three hundred internationally, have been assembling since 1812 to celebrate the work and life of the eighteenth-century Scottish poet Robert Burns with copious documentation of the author's writing and elaborate kilted dinners of haggis and whiskey, musical performances, and dramatic readings of Burns's poetry. Highland Societies in London and Edinburgh formed as early as the 1780s to preserve the symbolic artifacts of the Highland way of life. And the still functioning Saint Andrew's Societies, whose goal has been "to foster and encourage the love of Scotland, its history, literature, customs (including national athletic games)," were instrumental in beginning Highland Games in the nineteenth century throughout Canada and the United States. These organizations and their interest in preserving cultural ways, as they define them (language, art, sport, and dress), can be seen as the beginnings of what has become the heritage movement. Not only are the terms for maintaining Scottishness reproduced by recent club formations, but so, too, is the static focus on an "auld" Scottish culture that seems to have ended somewhere around the beginning of the nineteenth century.

However, there is a crucial difference between early Scottish organizations and present heritage nationality. Whereas Burns Clubs and St. Andrew's Societies were the very exclusive domain of high culture and elite, educated "gentlemen" (women were not admitted into Burns Clubs until 1909), Scottish heritage today is dramatically of a more popular movement. The broadened emphasis can be seen in the activity of Burns Clubs, which initially devoted most of their resources to "authenticating" the life of the poet through erecting public monuments, archiving manuscripts, recording criticism, composing Scots language dictionaries, and hosting reading competitions. While these activities still occur, the Burns Federation of Burns Clubs has produced a "Burns Heritage Collection" of gifts and memorabilia, some of which are "derived from original busts and paintings in the Burns Cottage Museum to give as close an association with the poet as possible."[61] I argue that it is this shift away from the "aura" of the original poet, and its restricted place in museums, libraries and private gatherings, towards the easily distributable mass-produced Burns-kitsch items that have popularized Scottishness and transformed it into heritage. This is not to say that through its popularization the Scottishness in Burns Clubs has become less or more authentic or that Burns' literary reputation has been cheapened. Rather, the way cultural authenticity is defined has moved in a different direction, towards a mediation of culture through commodity exchanges. Those wanting to "experience" the life and culture of the national bard, then, can still visit Scotland or read his work as people have done for almost two centuries. The difference is that now, an admirer (whether or not he or she is a member of the Burns Club) can participate in Scottishness by purchasing a whole line of clothing and accessories woven with "The Burns Heritage Check," a ball-point pen with the poet's profile, or cakes of honey soap packaged with the Burns Federation insignia. Commodity logic and kitsch items are fundamental to the construction of Scottish heritage, even in their literary forms.

The National Family: Scottish America's Blood Fantasies

Like the offer for the square foot of Ullapool land, what Scottishness is being preserved against (or what Scottishness *is*, for that matter) remains unstated. Implicitly, there is the distinct sense in heritage organizations that the essential ideals of the Scottish nation and Scottish historical identity are in jeopardy of being permanently lost and that club membership is an instrumental means to revitalizing the link to the past and the bond between people of "Scottish heritage." The presentation of national history is thus critical to Scottish heritage clubs to connect their members, with cultural origins that date back hundreds of years. What is clear, however, is that heritage's version of history invokes a national tradition of privilege by identifying with the accomplishments of elites and the drama of the winners, of conquest and the role of Scots in Britannia's imperial enterprise. Heritage histories commemorate the prosperity and might of colonial rule, as does the Scottish Tartans Society in using as its motto the words of a Scots general who, after watching the bloody defeat of a Punjabi regiment in 1857, sent his own men to seize an Indian rebel fortress: "Bring forrit the tartan: let my ain lads at them!" Lengthy narratives of legendary heroes, major textbook historical events, imperialist victories, artistic genius, and social prosperity are presented as foundations of Scottish identity that can be more fully accessed through a fifteen- to thirty-dollar annual membership to the "official" channels of a social group.

Clan Societies are particularly vibrant on this front, declaring their historical greatness as they sketch out the distinguished role of their ancestors in building a nation. Clan Donald USA, for example, describes its family roots reaching as far back as Scottish history itself:

> Clan Donald is one of the oldest, and probably the largest and most famous of all the Highland clans. Its Celtic heritage goes back to antiquity, beyond the 6th Century AD, to the great clans in what today is Ireland, Conn of the 100 Battles, Cairfre Raida, founder of Dal Raida in Antrim, Eire, and Colla Uathais. Our Viking heritage goes back to Ingiald "Ill-Ruler" and Olaf "Tree-Hewr" in the 7th Century Sweden and Norway. All of these traditional blood lines came together in the 12th Century Somerled MacGillebride MacGilladamnan, the historic founder of Clann Domhnaill. Our ancestors were regarded as the heads of the ancient race of Con, and the lineal heirs of the kings and Dalriadic Scots.[62]

Benedict Anderson calls this the "steady, solid simultaneity through time" that, in stretching across the eras, legitimizes ancestry and makes certain that its still evident roots are identical to those of the nation.[63] This construction by Clan Donald USA of national personhood then proceeds along a timeline of great moments, including the clan's part in fighting for the Scottish in the Battle of Bannockburn and the eighteenth-century Jacobite rebellions.[64] Not surprisingly, these two pivotal confrontations in the struggle for national autonomy appear in most clan histories; William Wallace and Robert the Bruce are frequently claimed as associates of a given clan in one form or another. And with the depictions of premodern, even prefeudal, clan life and its heraldry, the ideal is not quite the meek, happy, and pious Highlander, but as the Clan Urquhart Society illustrates, a militaristic, rugged, masculine, and dutiful clan-member: "The patriarchal system of clanship thus made the people regard, with unfailing devotion, their chief as the head of their race, and the representative of their common ancestor."[65]

Some clan histories extend even closer to the present, noting more recent achievements: "The Montgomery Clan produced the late Viscount Field Marshall Montgomery, the great tactician of the Second World War."[66] Sentiments of pride and distinction surrounding each clan's individual tartan, crest, and motto suggest a shared tie that connects each member to the originary source of nation, elevating the status of their individual identity by presuming that it comes from a "source" of greatness: "Clan Mackintosh is second to none. It's [*sic*] members have demonstrated that they are stalwart, fearless, and adventuresome people.... The Clan Mackintosh spirit is as strong as ever and binds our clansmen together in all parts of the world."[67] Periodic newsletters of activities, clan gatherings, scholarships for clan youths, genealogical services, clan "DNA Projects," and fundraising schemes thus dedicate themselves to preserving the evidence of this blood legacy.

Despite their claims to an uninterrupted order of historical clanship, the large-scale emergence of clan societies is an overwhelmingly recent phenomenon. Out of the nearly seventy organizations that include the date of their inception in their literature, all but thirteen were formed since 1970. But, by all indications, they have gained formidable popularity in just a few decades, no doubt partially due to the fact that it was not until 1984 that the Scottish Tourist Board won the right to market overseas directly, when before it relied on the resources of the British Tourist Authority.[68] Out of the more than 150 clan clubs, the 53 that have published their membership numbers alone comprise over 27,000 members internationally with larger organizations like the Clan Charmichael Society tallying over 3100.[69] What is clear is that the clan societies' emphasis on celebrating identity fits neatly with the emergence of heritage itself as a culturally viable category for imagining and accumulating the self.

If, as Benedict Anderson has argued, the formal universality of nation in the modern world has made it the case that everyone "has" a nationality,[70] the same might be said today of "heritage" and its claims to ancestral ties, historical cultures, ethnicities, and tribes which exist alongside one's nationality. Clan societies have become an effective arm of the heritage industry in making Scottishness an individually recognizable trait that, like nation, is shared, but also exclusive. For most clan societies, being a member of the club is restricted by the somewhat arbitrary laws of lineage and descent, which refer to the inherited privileges of blood, culture and ethnicity. Having the name of the clan is officiated by the genealogical services and archives that virtually every organization provides, and, in some cases (as with the Bell Family Association's required "Pedigree Chart"), even serve as a gatekeeper for those who may claim the name, but are not "really" of Scottish descent — or at least, are unable to prove it. With eligibility comes the distinction of legitimizing one's heritage and of becoming "true" members of a living historical kinship: "Clanship is a family matter that transcends nationality, and we regard ourselves as an extended family."[71] For a few organizations, memberships are available (for the usual annual fee) to those who do not meet the standard requirement of bearing the surname of the clan in one its variant spellings or of having the name of a clan "bardic sept," a historical affiliate of the family. These "associate memberships," when extended, are given those who show "demonstrated enthusiasm" according to the Clan Cameron of North American, even though they do not have the name or other genealogical proof.[72] Those who "have" the identity are granted automatic membership. Those who don't must prove that they are worthy enough to be included, as if they are being naturalized into the nation of Scottishness.

The loose usage of the terms of kinship, family, and original lines of folk ancestry reveals perhaps the most obviously troubling effect of clan societies' construction of Scottish heritage. The brand of cultural and national interest that clan organizations seem to be interested in preserving is white ethnicity, an identity of racial privilege that is both exclusive and biologically defined. Inasmuch as clan heritage is an identification with a national "family," in today's cultural politics in Canada, the United States, and Great Britain, it cannot be ignored that clan societies are also the celebration of the patriarchal traditions and the origins of whiteness. Women are not only rendered largely invisible in favor of masculine heroics of historical warriors — and their modern equivalent, entrepreneurs — but the clan becomes an analog for heterosexual union, moral purity, and male control. Clan mottos, war cries, and battle reenactments at Clan gatherings reinforce the idea that the "family" is preserved and protected through masculine displays of brute strength and militarism. Or, as in the description from the Clan Armstrong's activities at a Highland Games in Florida, women help reenact the old systems of women's work: "This was a recreated medieval village highlighting various crafts including stone cutting (want a full size Celtic cross?); sword and weapons making; etc. One woman held an angora rabbit in her lap and was pulling hair from the hare and spinning it into yarn." Clan activity is not just where conservative traditions of family thrive, but also where they seem to begin: "A couple was married at the games in ancient dress to a traditional Scottish ceremony. There was nary a dry eye."[73]

In the U.S., the traditions invoked by Scottish heritage societies have also helped promote an assertion of white ethnicity during a period of general anxiety about the gains people of color have made in demanding their place in the cultural and political mainstream. Matthew Frye Jacobson has identified the post-civil rights 1970s and '80s in the U.S. as a time of "ethnic revival" when new distinctions among white people were ideologically articulated, allowing groups to prove themselves to be not *that* white because they belonged to a particular ethnicity. He describes the movement as

> an impulse whose energy derived from a distinctly "white" set of grievances and entitlements, but whose central tendency was to disavow "whiteness" in favor of group narratives that measured their distance from WASP mainstream, or even, in some instances, that dwelt upon oppression under the heel of Nordic America.[74]

The result, Jacobson argues, is that "new ethnics" emerge to protest against accusations that as white people they enjoy the structural benefits of racial privilege, by pointing out their own marginalization in history as an oppressed people. They are then transformed by whites from "Caucasians," a category which has lost its political currency in American public debates, to Scots, Letts, Poles, French, or Greeks. This is not to say that these white ethnicities were ever erased or that the real prejudices they may have endured upon entering the hostile cauldron known as the melting pot were forgotten. Rather, their ethnic identities became less socially meaningful as they became included as "whites." The problem, as Jacobson argues, is that upon the reclamation of white ethnicity, considerations of race and the relationship of these groups to racialized nonwhite ethnicities — Afro-Caribbean Islanders, Latinos, Native Americans — are abandoned as ethnicity is abstracted from its context of whiteness and the structural realities of racial subordination. According to Mary Waters, as an "optional ethnicity," white heritage posits all identities to be equally interchangeable, and in doing so fundamentally devalues the qualitative ethnic and racial inequalities that shape social life.[75]

Similar tensions are described by Stuart Hall concerning Britain during the same period, as "new ethnicities" within groups of color asserted themselves in culture and politics. Being "black" was complicated by historical differences that challenged simple hegemonic race classification of white/not-white through the cultural specificity of being Pakistani, Afro-Caribbean, or Bengali in Great Britain. In response, vicious forms of "Englishness" emerged on similar terms by declaring its need to be recognized as a legitimate ethnic category of national "heritage" along with groups struggling to be represented. Dislodged from the structural inequities of racism in Britain, English ethnicity was articulated as one among many, but, not coincidentally, as one most aligned with the nation: its "first" and oldest.[76] As Hall explains, the energy around this white ethnicity in the "New Times" platform of British conservatism in the seventies and eighties is nothing less than a politicized effort to align the nation with essential ethnic origins that reclaim the nation for its white populace:

> [Thatcherism] has powerfully organized itself around particular forms of patriarchy and cultural or national identity. Its defense of "Englishness," of that way of "being British" or of the English feeling "Great again," is a key to some of the unexpected sources of Thatcherism's popularity. Cultural racism has been one of its most powerful, enduring, effective — and least remarked — sources of strength. For that very reason, "Englishness," as a privileged and restrictive cultural identity, is becoming a site of contestation for those many marginalized ethnic and racial groups in the society who feel excluded by it and who hold to a different form of racial and ethnic identification and insist on cultural diversity as a goal of society in New Times.[77]

Although Hall does not use the term "whiteness" as Jacobson does, his analysis of Englishness runs to the heart of how white identity is not just an ethnic difference, but a white-supremacist one. These ethnicities, which exist as part of the socially privileged "white race," have undoubtedly been contingent upon the displacement, dispossession, and subordination of other ethnicities — most acutely, against groups of color.

As I have argued in Chapter Two, claims to Englishness have also been aimed at Scots and other "Celtic" groups — Welsh and Irish — through ethnic nationalist arguments which position English culture as the rightful center of Great Britain. Yet, as Paul Gilroy argues, the primary difference associated with belonging to a "true" Britishness in the last three decades (at the very least) has not so much been drawn between England and the regional cultures of Scotland, Wales and Northern Ireland, but between British whites and British "blacks," as non-whites are shut out of the cultural fold: "[T]he word 'immigrant' became synonymous with the word 'black' during the 1970s. It is still felt today as black settlers and their British-born children are denied authentic national membership on the basis of their 'race' and, at the same time, prevented from aligning themselves within the 'British race' on the grounds that their national allegiance inevitably lies elsewhere."[78] While it should not be denied that cultural prejudices still exist against non–English whites, the political terrain of difference has shifted considerably to make national inclusion across Britain a question of being *not* "black," however this has been defined.

Anne McClintock's analysis of the changing scientific and cultural categorization of race traces these shifts to the nineteenth-century height of

British colonization. The "Celts," a group once understood as an inferior race to the English within Britain, were transformed from being racially different to being ethnically different as white identity helped consolidate Britain by aligning race and nation. Asserting a unified and biologically justified national civilization over and against colonized peoples often made the differences between mainly middle- and upper-class Scots and English less significant in the colonies where racial distinctions served to enforce British rule.[79] In the twentieth century similar tactics were used to exclude immigrants on British soil who, at one time or another, had arrived from formerly colonized sites in Asia, Africa, and the West Indies. In many ways, this is also the argument that Noel Ignatiev offers in his study *How the Irish Became White*, about the nineteenth-century U.S. Irish immigrants and their children who transformed themselves from members of a racially inferior group to "authentic" whites by defining themselves against slaves and freed blacks and actively supporting their subordination.

Yet, as those who have investigated the history of Irish immigrants in Britain and the United States have demonstrated, Scots in both sites were eager to point out they were *not* Irish, but British. According to Carl Wittke, the category of "Scotch-Irish," a term unknown in Ireland, was invented by Scottish Americans to distinguish descendants of the first wave of Irish immigrants — many of whom had lived in Ulster and most of whom came from landowning Presbyterian families of Scottish descent — from the great influx of mainly Catholic Irish later in the nineteenth century who were understood as racially and religiously inferior.[80] Accompanying the logic of racial difference, however, are the clear class distinctions that explain how being Scottish in the United States and Canada was associated with positions of privilege. Whereas most Irish emigrated as poor laborers in the nineteenth century, Scots émigrés who moved to North America, especially before 1813, were property owners from the middle class seeking to increase their influence and wealth, so much so that in considering the presence of Scots in territories claimed by England, historian Theodore Allen has called Scottish lowlanders "junior partners in the English colonization."[81] The movement out of Scotland to North America in the first half of the nineteenth century was fostered by strong personal and family links that in many cases made relocation to settlements in Canada or the Southern states of the U.S. as easy, in terms of material and community support from formal and informal sources, as the much shorter move to London.[82] Commercial and social organizations like the North British Society of Nova Scotia (1790–1812), for instance, were not uncommon in setting up employment opportunities and relief funds for new and impoverished Scots immigrants.[83]

Even after the Scottish clearances which forced poor agrarian Highlanders to look for employment abroad later in the nineteenth century, a whole other class of Scots was moving with money in hand looking for new land enterprises and industrial markets. Scottish investors between 1789 and 1888, for example, financed two-thirds of the cattle ranches in the American west, and the City of Glasgow Bank financed much of the Western Union Railroad, which ran from Lake Michigan to the Mississippi. By 1896 Scottish investment in American expansion was to the order of £60 million.[84] In terms of enjoying both the racial and economic privileges in immigration, the Scots were not an oppressed group that suffered the kind of discrimination dealt to Irish, Italian, Portuguese and other immigrants at one time castigated for their linguistic, religious, and racial otherness, though now socially categorized as white. The middle-class character of the Scottish in North America made assimilation into the Anglicized hegemony relatively easy and supported the kind of perceptions that Neal Dow, Maine entrepreneur, publicly expressed in 1880: "Of all immigrants to our country the Scotch are always the most welcome. They bring us muscle and brain and tried skill and trust-worthiness of which they are managers of the most successful ones."[85] The trope of the "Lad o Pairts" Scot, whose innate talent catapults him from peasant beginnings into great professional success, seems to be projected onto all Scots as class privileges are conflated with industriousness. Even further, the economic parochialism of "helping your own" culture becomes understood ethnic superiority.

Now, over a hundred years later, similar arguments in heritage nationalism for the historical greatness of Scottish "stock" remain completely devoid of the material conditions that have ensured social successes for whites of "Scots ancestry." This is certainly the spirit behind the 1996 history *The Mark of the Scots: Their Astonishing Contributions to History, Science, Democracy, Literature, and the Arts*. Published in the United States and written by an American, its goal to "inform the world of the intellectual might that has surged out from the glens and made such a rich contribution to civilization"[86] takes shape in a comprehensive "who's who" list of how Scots have shaped all that is good in Western culture and the world. Throughout its over 350 pages, it attributes the origins of present civilization to the noteworthy individuals in virtually every cultural field, especially in the United States, since it is "to a great extent, a Scottish creation, born largely of Scottish ideas and efforts"

(4) and exists as "the most powerful nation of all time and the model for the foundation of countless countries and government." As if it were tallying points at an Olympics of history, categories are given a "score" showing, for example, that the 21 of 56 men who signed the Declaration of Independence "is a score of 38 percent, versus the 6.7 percent representation of Scots in the general population in 1790" (269), or that the 45 of 416 Nobel prize-winners of Scottish ancestry yields "almost one of every nine awards, for a score of 10.8 percent" (295), or the 31 out of 41 American presidents, "a score of more than 75 percent, and when compared with less than 4.4 percent of the American people in general who are of Scottish descent amounts to an overrepresentation of more than 17 times" (272). Along with a "Proposed Scottish-American All-Time All Star [Baseball] Team," we also learn that such unlikely figures as e.e. cummings (who "spelled his name in a distinctive way and came from a family which claimed descent from the Red Comyn" [203]), Elvis Presley ("descended from Andrew Presley, who had come to America from Scotland two centuries before" [243]), Audrey Hepburn ("born in Holland to a father who was descended from James Hepburn, fourth earl of Bothwell, one of the husbands of Mary, Queen of Scots" [252]), and the founders of MacDonald's hamburgers (while being Irish-American, "Most of the Irish McDonald's ultimately descended from Scottish galloglasses" [285–6]),[87] all have Scottish ancestry in some form or another. As with clan societies, what counts as being of Scottish heritage is broadly defined, sometimes relying on genealogical records, sometimes on surname, and sometimes on claims of the individuals or their biographers. The assumptions are many and not difficult to dismantle logically or historically: most notably, name equates to ancestry; the Irish, or at least a huge portion of them, are *really* Scottish; and once you have been identified as having "one-drop" of Scottish blood, you are nothing else.

What lies behind this history of the most bizarre sort is more than just an explicitly stated pride in the achievements of "Scots." It is an ethnic supremacism justified by both a simplistic reactionary reading of the "best and brightest" in western culture and evidence of biological inheritance. The implicit, and at times not-so-implicit, organizing theme of the text is that the ancestral bloodlines of Scotland have created better people. The opening paragraph of the text says as much:

> Somewhere within the depths of all of us who are of Scottish blood, there is a knowledge that despite our dispersion throughout the continents and our constantly increasing assimilation into other nations, we are still somehow one people,

Chapter Five

HEROES, THUGS AND LEGENDS

Celluloid Scotland at Century's End

Just months after Tony Blair's Labor Party had completed its landmark May 1997 shutout of the long-standing Conservative Party in Scotland, it faced its first challenge from the powerful populism of the tartan monster. In mid–February of 1998, film superstar Sean Connery — alias the original James Bond seven times over and 1987 Academy Award winner, alias *People Magazine's* Sexiest Man in 1989 and *New Woman's* "Sexiest Man of the Century," alias the Scottish National Party's most influential public and financial supporter, and alias Scotland's indisputably most famous international face — was denied knighthood for "contributions to the arts" by Britain's new government. In what was quickly becoming a public relations nightmare, word spread that an intervention from another Scot — and a powerful Scot at that — Scottish Secretary and Labor Party member Donald Dewar had derailed Connery's nomination. The results were predictable: opinion polls reported the SNP's highest-ever rating, support for Labor had dipped seven percentage points,[1] speculation abounded about how such a trend might secure a majority of party nationalists in the upcoming inaugural Scottish Parliament elections,[2] and headlines screamed "Connery Denied Knighthood over Scots Nationalist Links,"[3] "Knighthood Snub Was Political, Says Connery,"[4] and "Connery 'Stabbed in the Back,'"[5] suggesting a Labor conspiracy against an advocate of Scottish independence. *The Scottish Mirror* also devoted over five pages to its campaign for Connery.[6] In response, Labor Party members were obliged to defend the decision, citing the movie star's tax exile status in Marbella, Spain, and his controversial comments made over the years in interviews, including one in a 1985 issue of *Vanity Fair* where he maintained that there are occasions when it is appropriate for a man to slap a woman.

It became clear that the denial of the nation's most highly recognized cultural icon into Britain's most exclusive club was a denial of Scotland itself. A *System Three* opinion poll revealed that, regardless of Labor's reasons and Dewar's rejections of conspiracy theories, 59 percent of Scots believed Connery should have received the honor.[7] While the Labor government had won over Scotland in the May 1997 elections by campaigning for "Home-Rule" initiatives — previously the province only of official nationalists — it had not anticipated simmering resentments over centuries of Scotland's cultural marginality. A Scottish Parliament with its own tax-levying powers made sense economically and appealed to Scots who shared a sense of what Tom Nairn has called a more pragmatic "civic," rather than cultural, nationalism. But the rapid swing in public opinion towards the home-grown SNP and away from a Westminster-based ruling government indicated that popular representations of Scottish culture, especially those possessing the international cachet of Connery, mattered to Scots as much as fiscal policy. The affair reeked of yet another Prime Minister "not in touch" with the Scottish people.[8]

Despite the fact that Connery's success and notoriety have been more the product of Hollywood than Scotland, or that the first Mr. Bond has lived more of his life in the Costa del Sol and the Bahamas than in his self-proclaimed "homeland," the response to his derailment from the fast track to peerage illustrates that he became, and remains still, a cultural hero who represents a valued image of Scottish identity. Connery's cinematic fame both at home and abroad and his purported betrayal by the court and crown are not just a Scot-done-wrong-story, but an illustration of the way in which film and film figures play an important role in the perception of Scottish cultural identity, national prowess, and historical worth. The presence of films about Scotland, as well as those produced in Scotland, reached its most dynamic point in the 1990s with three blockbusters in three years — *Braveheart*, *Rob Roy* and *Trainspotting* — earning eleven Academy Award nominations between them and taking home five Oscars. Accompanying their box office success was the international attention they drew to the spectacular vision of Scottish local landscape, legend, history, language, literature and contemporary social reality that only the cinema can provide. As David Bruce, the former Director of the Scottish Film Council, has suggested, if there had been a 1996 Oscar for best supporting country, Scotland would have won.[9]

As with the institution that has become the Scottish heritage industry, discussed in the previous chapter, film in Scotland is an increasingly central site in which the Scottish nation is produced, in the imagination of Scots filmmakers and American screenwriters and directors, as well as in the perceptions of a broad transatlantic audience. While public resources have been increasingly channeled by the Scottish Office into Scottish film projects, as well as into special funds and tax incentives to foreign film companies, the distinctly American brand of Hollywood imagery and marketing strategy have become major partners in the construction of cultural narratives of, and about, Scottish identity. Indeed, heritage identity has contributed to and benefited from depictions of the heroic Highlander, which have been fundamental to the colorful *Braveheart* and *Rob Roy* versions of the Scottish past. Despite the shoddy history of William Wallace in *Braveheart*, the biggest of all "Scottish" movies, and its liberal, if not altogether peculiar use of the Scots dialect, or the fact that a majority of its production staff, actors, writers, and business partners were clearly *not* Scottish, the film and its images are frequently used by Scots to promote the nation's culture: in politics, the 1996 Scottish National Party exploited the familiar movie-poster figure of a dramatically tartaned and battle-wearied Mel Gibson in a campaign bill that read, "We Need Independence Now More Than Ever!" In tourism, the Stirling travel board advertises its region today as "Braveheart Country," and another boasts "Rob Roy Roamed Here and So Can You and Your Family." In national policy, the Scottish Office has cited the success of the epic as reason for accelerating official support for film, including appointing a "scout" in Hollywood from the Scottish Screen Locations committee to promote the benefits to production companies of shooting in Scotland.[10] The SNP's party platform includes "considering film finance and the potential for attracting incoming production, and encouraging indigenous work."[11] And, in less official contexts, the annual "Braveheart Conference" convenes hundreds of *Braveheart* fans for three days at Stirling Castle to celebrate the film and to offer tribute to William Wallace's legacy, no doubt part of the reason that the annual visitors to the Wallace monument increased from 66,000 to 167,000 the year after *Braveheart*'s release.[12]

The increased attention to film has not only come from audiences' hunger for the Scottish national home, but is also the product of governmental interventions in the late eighties and early nineties. The Scottish Film Production Fund doubled its budget from £340,000 to £735,000 between 1994 and 1996 (and gave substantial support to *Rob Roy*[13]), and major constitutional changes in the Scottish Film Council made it an independent body able to oversee agencies such as Scottish Screen Locations and Scottish Film Training. More recently, the Scottish Office rode the success of Highland Hollywood, or what has been termed the "*Braveheart* Effect," in centralizing the four primary bodies of Scottish film — the Scottish Film Council, the Scottish Film Production Fund, Scottish Screen Locations and Scottish Broadcast and Film Training — into the Scottish Screen Agency in order to financially aid and promote film production.

The national image of Scotland generated by celluloid Scotland and the Big Three of 1990s Scottish film — *Braveheart, Rob Roy* and *Trainspotting* — replicates a recurring tradition in Scottish cultural representation that counterposes narratives of legend and fantasy in *Braveheart* and *Rob Roy* against the raw dystopic realism of contemporary working-class life that is so evident in *Trainspotting*. As a group, they reproduce in many ways one of the major tensions of Scottish Renaissance literature I explore in Chapter 2 between Neil Gunn's romanticized landscapes and Lewis Grassic Gibbon's portraits of industrial squalor. And, like their Scottish Renaissance predecessors, the Big Three films have done nothing to challenge the notion that national historic change belongs to the world of men and their machinations. Each film speaks directly to specific ideals of a contemporary Scottish masculinity that are heavily reliant on nationalist sentiments of a proud and passionate "Scottish nature," anti–English portrayals of gratuitously caricatured London aristocrats, and highly sexualized Scottish madonnas.

As most critics and viewers have been eager to note, *Trainspotting* stands apart from the others' gratuitous militarism and "Auld Scotland" nostalgia. Its sympathetic and carefully nuanced portrayal of heroin addiction, like the '70s and '80s Glasgow industrial "Clydeside" fiction of James Kelman, and Archie Hinds, is consciously posed against the prevailing tourist-driven image of romantic Scotland. Nevertheless, as I argue below, there are important continuities running through these texts, despite their narrative and representational contrasts. While *Trainspotting*'s humanizing focus on the social ciphers of Scotland is refreshing, the film, like *Braveheart* and *Rob Roy*, centers almost exclusively on the lives of men who struggle heroically to transcend their social strictures through acts of brute violence and aggression. *Trainspotting* is certainly less sure than the others about the hope of its hero's victory, but nonetheless it reproduces the notion that the redefinition of national identity occurs between men who battle against state intervention, the rape of their women, corruption by effeminate (English) men, the destruction of Scottish mothers, and the provincial narrowness of their Scottish peers. However, Nira

Yuval-Davis explains that these familiar social conventions of national sovereignty, abundantly evident in war zones across the globe that threaten women's lives, *depend* on women's expressions, their sexuality, and their bodies as boundary markers of the hetero-normative national family — violently crossed, penetrated, defended, and controlled — through which patriarchy and military rule negotiate and authorize their imminence. Structurally supporting these narratives of ethnic pride, cultural justice, or individual heroism is a misogynistic national home relegating women to the role of passive victims who are introduced only to be admired for their effluvial femininity and then eliminated, either literally by their death, or by a plotline that no longer finds them necessary. In sum, Hollywood Scotland centers on the most conservative of male concerns about the loss of the "freedom," "honor," and "bravery" that, when examined more closely, reveal the contemporary anxieties of the most privileged members of society about the loss of economic movement, male control, and the cultural traditions of national "unity" that undergird their authority.

Nationalism Shaken Not Stirred

The response to Connery's snubbed knighthood by the general populace and local politicians deserves more explanation because it draws attention to the tenuous bonds between Scotland and England that hold "British" culture together. More importantly, in the minds of many Scots, the events redrew the boundaries historically separating the two nations and brought into relief a structure of power in which, when all is said and done, England has the final word — and that word was an authoritative "no." On one level, this equation — one nation rejecting the values of another — is convincing: the ruling party in London demonstrated its collusion with English interests and denied Scotland's prodigal son his rightful place amongst the queen's honorees. The press echoed this formulation, reporting that the "purely political" motives of Westminster were designed to embarrass the seemingly objective and apolitical achievements of the Scottish actor.[14] However, such a crude premise of the "purely political" does little to account for the multiple factors that contributed to the way the Connery affair was executed and how the scandal was understood in Scotland.

Besides the fact that Connery is a Scot who has achieved fame in movies, his popularity in Scotland can also attributed to his outspoken nationalism, visually summed up by the tattoo "Scotland Forever" printed on his arm. He has been an open supporter and the biggest vote-winner of the SNP since 1991 (the party's popularity jumped seven points when he declared his support on television),[15] participating in campaign ads, appearing in Party literature, and reportedly contributing £50,000 annually to its coffers. But it was not the SNP that the Scottish public felt had been unjustly betrayed; after all, at the time of the knighthood snub, almost three times as many people in Scotland supported parties other than the SNP. Rather, it was an image of Scottishness that had been disrespected, a living picture of the "Lad O' Pairts" working-class Edinburgh boy from the Fountainbridge slums who began his career as a milkman at age thirteen and then advanced through the ranks to become the famed face of Scottish talent.

David Bruce's catalogue of Scottish film begins its description of Connery by citing the *Baseline Encyclopedia of Film*: "Dashing, charismatic, and effortlessly masculine leading man who successfully escaped the profitable straight [*sic*] jacket of James Bond to become one of the most beloved and respected stars of contemporary Hollywood."[16] Indeed, Connery represents not only a Scot who has achieved at the highest levels of fame and wealth, but a Scot who has set the bar in defining international ideals of mainstream masculinity, from his early roles as the suave undercover Cold Warrior to his more recent parts as an austere and graying grandfather. As the above description suggests, it is not 007 that made Connery, but Connery's "effortlessly masculine" qualities that made 007. Still more, he is the example of a Scot who proved on-screen he could be a more convincing and a more sexually appealing English gentleman than anyone the English themselves had to offer, whether that was as James Bond or as legendary English kings Arthur (*First Knight*) and Richard the Lionhearted (*Robin Hood: Prince of Thieves*). The players on the other side of this knighthood narrative were the dour and bookish figure of Dewar, dubbed by the press as "Dr. NO," and the Edinburgh-schooled, but obviously English, Tony Blair, both of whom endorsed the knighthood of Elton John, the openly gay and cross-dressing English glam pop star whose most recent achievement included a smash-hit elegy to Princess Diana. The impression was that Scotland's very hero of manhood had been publicly emasculated, once again, by England.

As an icon of Scottishness, Connery can be seen as Hollywood's contribution to heritage identity, as it blurs the distinction between Connery-the-man and the characters he plays on screen. That is, Connery's suave image is both a product of the world of fantasy and an example of a real image of Scottish life, appearing in literature like Irvine Welsh's novel *Trainspotting* as a dream of a manly working-class hero. And, as the Scottish public's response indicates, this fantasy has real purchase in national life. Despite the actor's self-proclaimed investment in the future of Scotland, however, it is impossible to ignore the realities of his own life that contradict the depth of his commitment. As noted earlier, Connery hasn't actually lived in Scotland for four decades, opting instead for estates in the Bahamas, Spain, and Los Angeles. Moreover, he has appeared in advertisements for Japanese — not Scotch — whiskey distilleries. He claims to have a political commitment to the principles of citizenship but has stayed out of politics in the national and local communities where he actually resides. And finally, despite numerous efforts, Connery still has not been able to adequately redress the alarming comments he made in advocating the violence against women.[17] A point that seems to have been forgotten altogether is that while Connery showed public disappointment at being passed over, as a policy the SNP does not approve of British honors, encouraging members to refuse them and barring officeholders from accepting peerage. One SNP council member wrote a letter to *The Times* stating, "[W]e should be delighted Sean Connery has been ignored."[18]

Yet these contradictions seem to have been less important to the public than Connery's contributions to their perception of Scottish talent. They are ignored in much the same way that national history has given way to national heritage, as I demonstrate in Chapter Four, wherein national identity is removed from a consistent commitment to a community, place, or civic participation within it and is replaced by a framework almost exclusively invested in the ability of individuals to perform a national character on their own terms. Overshadowing Connery's severe lack of involvement in Scottish life are his Scots accent and a gratuitously nationalistic tattoo, an unfailing machismo, and a reported £50 million net worth, a significant portion of which has been channeled as lavish contributions to the SNP. Together these characteristics make Connery one of Scotland's favored sons, a "free agent" whose "heritage" and ability to declare Scottishness, as he has defined it, allow him to be at once an everyday Scot, permanently on the "home team," as well as a player on any other national team he chooses.

At the same time, this is not a case of the public merely being duped by Hollywood imagery or Scottish politics, but rather an indication of a real distrust of how Scottish culture and its heroes, especially those in the popular media, are judged by England and the Scottish intelligentsia. Not only do few movie superstars enter into official politics with as heavy a hand as Connery has extended to a specific party, but even fewer living images of national identity advocate so actively and openly a specific political platform. In this way the knighthood snub is also a rejection of a perceived man of conscience who really does not *have* to speak for Scotland, but "courageously" does so at the risk of public humiliation. In other words, Connery represents the Scot who stands up for the nation for no other purpose than for the "love" of his country, from no other position of interest except his duty as a Scot, and motivated by nothing other than his heart. Appearing in a political television broadcast for the SNP, Connery nearly quoted verbatim Mel Gibson's William Wallace in *Braveheart* in proclaiming, "We fight not for glory nor for wealth nor honors, but only and alone we fight for freedom."[19] This is not just life imitating art, as I argue in the rest of this chapter, but the largely reactionary cultural narrative of the hero leading the nation to its own conscience. What constitutes "freedom" remains a mystery, especially from the lips of a multi-millionaire tax exile, except as a form of reductive anti–Englishness that poses an absolutely unified Scotland against an equally unified, abusive, and even enslaving, political overlord of English government. There is a hint of Blair's declaration in a September 1999 speech to his New Labor party that the "Class War" was over, but the fight against "inequality" had just begun. Systematic social divisions of class privilege, joblessness, patriarchy, and ethnic strife be damned, what matters most is the neo-liberal view that individuals, especially the well-off ones like Connery, be equally "free" to acquire wealth without suffering from the prejudiced attitudes of others.[20] If we were to correct the people with bad hearts, it seems, the playing field would be equalized. As a whole, it is the prevailing image of an individualized Scottish nationality and a slightly politicized heritage identity, fostered by cultural icons like Connery and reproduced by Hollywood's infotainment version of the nation's history.

Bravehearts and Bedwetters

American film critic, Joseph Roquemore, echoes the mainstream reaction to *Braveheart* in his 1999 movie guide about popular cinematic recreations of historical events:

> *Braveheart* doesn't claim infallibility for historical accuracy — as it shouldn't, since scholars are uncertain about many details of Wallace's life. But it gives us the next best thing; stunning period detail, great battle scenes, firmly drawn characters, and

try £1.7 million, *Trainspotting*, offered an alternative and dismal picture of Scottish life. Set in the contemporary Leith slums of Edinburgh, the story of five twenty-something men and their drug scores, barroom brawls, sexual disasters, and run-ins with the law, tossed images of heroic Scotland right into the North Sea. If *Braveheart* and *Rob Roy* construct the national body as reinforcing the boundaries of Scotland's strength and unequivocal sovereignty, *Trainspotting* represents a body that has been so fully penetrated that autonomy — national or individual — is put permanently into question. The collective body in view is spiked by the drug needle, infected with the AIDS virus, numbed by consumer culture, politically detached, morally corrupt, addicted, bored, disloyal, depressed, and thoroughly vulnerable to the influences that disrupt the possibility of any kind of independence. The nihilism of the film is palpable, as self-mutilation and gratuitous, unprovoked violence signal a surrender to a dystopic culture that systematically generates the conditions of poverty, immediate gratification, alienated labor, and psychic isolation.

This everyday underbelly of Scottish life is not quite a dirty realist presentation serving as a corrective of cultural myths, but a highly stylized, often comic, and playfully hip film that reverberates between frank images of addiction's hardcore consequences and amusing surrealist fantasies. It may nowadays be an academic cliché to suggest a film technically takes on music-video characteristics, but in the case of *Trainspotting*, this claim could be no more appropriate. Opening with a five-and-a-half-minute montage, accompanied by the thumping punk-rock background of Iggy Pop, the film introduces over half of the entire film's cast as it juggles fragments of five spatially and temporally disjointed scenes, all held together by the verbal assault of the main character's witty monologue and the uninterrupted edgy musical score. It was perhaps this technique that inspired Miramax to buy distributing rights to the Scottish-grown small-budget film and invest millions to market a movie about heroin addicts to an international popular audience; Polygram spent £750,000 in selling the film to British consumers alone.[27] The difficult question about *Trainspotting* and its construction of Scottish life lies in the common-sense contradiction of a film that focuses on the dour conditions of junkie life and at the same time gives such pleasure to mainstream viewers and industry experts.

Despite its rejections of the grand narratives of the nation's bonnie past and future and the film's efforts to expose the irrelevance of these traits to a real portion of Scotland's population, *Trainspotting*'s irreverent and sweeping cultural critique is so trapped by its own cynicism that in the end it affirms the hero of global culture: the young freewheeling upwardly mobile male corporate punk. The models of Rob Roy and William Wallace may no longer be adequate, but the new body of contemporary Scotland and its main character Mark Renton (Ewan MacGregor) illustrate that a quick-witted and boyishly handsome subject of culture can work the system, escape to find success in London, and finesse his way out of the social confines that are poverty, addiction, and Scotland itself. Not to mention the other burdens that seem to be his friends and family, who remain trapped by their own Scottish identities. In other words, *Trainspotting* complicates and shifts some of the boundaries of the historic manly warrior and legend-hero in the national home, but only insofar as a cutting-edge, highly individualized, mobile, yet still clearly masculinized figure of culture takes his place.

As the opening scene and its musical accompaniment illustrate, the film is framed by the punk ethos as Renton and Spud (Ewen Bremner) frantically run from two security guards in stride with the pounding acoustic drum of Iggy Pop's "Lust for Life." Yet the film is not a just a story about urban delinquents. When a car pulls out in front of Renton and flips him over the hood, the main character gets up not to continue his flight, but to stare down the driver through the windshield and, in an arrested moment of startling detachment, to break into crazed laughter. Perhaps a guttersnipe variation of the Beatles' intro to *A Hard Day's Night* where the Fab Four are gleefully pursued by squealing girls, the movie recalls punk's thrill of enacting its contempt for authority — both that of the police and that of the sensible and successful sporty-sedan owners of the world — and the pleasure of maintaining a kinetic balance between a legitimate sneering counterculture and outright criminality. Greil Marcus describes the punk ethos as a politics of negation, marked by its tools of real and symbolic violence, blasphemy, cacophonous dissipation, absurdity, pranks, and sardonic smiles aimed at virtually everything it came in contact with:

> The very emptiness of the terrain [punks] had cleared — the multiplication of new voices from below, the intensification of abuse from above, both sides fighting for possession of that suddenly cleared ground — had pushed them toward self-destruction, into the silence of a nihilist noise.[28]

The politics of punk, which Marcus traces from the Sex Pistols and the Buzzcocks to an earlier century's worth of largely male avant-gardist traditions including Dada, Situationism and Lettrism, involved hyperbolic performances that attempted to both highlight and disrupt, at least temporarily, the hierarchies, bureaucracies, and structures of alienation of proper society.

Trainspotting's embrace of Iggy Pop, one of the 1970s punk movement's last currently producing musical icons, and the film's opening chase-scene monologue appear almost as an end-of-the-century restatement of punk sensibilities and their rejection of mainstream success, consumer values, and self-help narratives:

> Choose life. Choose a job. Choose a career. Choose a family. Choose a fucking big television, choose washing machines, cars, compact disc players and electrical tin openers. Choose good health, low cholesterol and dental insurance. Choose fixed-interest mortgage repayments. Choose a starter home. Choose your friends. Choose leisurewear and matching luggage. Choose a three-piece suite on hire purchase in a range of fucking fabrics. Choose DIY and wonderin' who the fuck you are on a Sunday morning. Choose sitting on that couch watching mind-numbing, spirit-crushing game shows, stuffing fucking junk food into your mouth. Choose rotting away at the end of it all, pishing your last in a miserable home, nothing more than an embarrassment to the selfish, fucked-up brats you have spawned to replace yourself. Choose your future. Choose life.
>
> But why would I want to do a thing like that?
>
> I chose not to choose life: I chose something else. And the reasons? There are no reasons. Who needs reasons when you've got heroin?

The verbal barrage, more like a violent spasm of ironized commercial slogans, middle-class nuclear family fantasies and bootstraps philosophies, is both a rejection and an embrace of society's total cooptation by bourgeois leisure life. The implicit "you" of each sentence suggests a depersonalized and monolithic voice of middle-class culture that commands a choice be made. And like Renton's diatribe, this demand for a "choice" is so persistent that in its repetitious urgency, it becomes uniform and monotonous. It is thoroughly emptied of its possibility for providing a real differentiated option. Life, the future, and even health, are so equated with time-saver commodities, sensible fashion, boredom, loneliness, and existential angst, that the only choice is a rejection of choice altogether, since an increasingly angry ("fucking") negation of one means the ("fucking") negation of all: "I chose not to choose life." Much like the Sex Pistols' anthematic chorus "No Future for You!," the "choice" of life in the monologue suggests that the only alternative is not quite death, but a transitory anti-life of irrational, self-destructive, and socially unacceptable pleasures.

At least temporarily, the distrust of mainstream discourses of self-growth and social progress is important in reimagining Scotland because it also draws attention to the role that nationalist cultural myths play in propagating these narratives of middle-class achievement. The cues that mark *Trainspotting* as a film about life in Scotland are primarily confined to a range of thick Scottish accents and the use of distinctively Scots words like "radge" and "swedge," which made for a linguistic challenge to non–Scottish audiences. The film was forced to use subtitles for one scene, and many scenes in the American version were completely redubbed. A brief hiking trip to a desolate moor in the country to get "fresh air" and a taste of "the great outdoors," according to Tommy (Kevin McKidd), for three of the other principal characters, Renton, Spud, and Sick Boy (Johnny Lee Miller), directly answers the question Tommy poses, "Doesn't it make you proud to be Scottish?" Renton's answer is a predictably unequivocal rejection:

> It's shite being Scottish! We're the lowest of the fucking low, the scum of the earth, the most wretched, miserable, servile, pathetic trash that was ever shat into civilization. Some people hate the English. I don't. They're just wankers. We, on the other hand, are colonized by wankers. We can't even pick a decent culture to be colonized by. We are ruled by effete arseholes. It's a shite state of affairs to be in, Tommy, and all the fresh air in the world will not make any fucking difference.

The notion that Scotland is a wee dear green place is shattered by an angry, self-loathing blast against the bankrupt promise of a proud national identity. Voicing one of the most popular of Scottish traditions, Tommy's appeal to romantic nationalism and the inspiration of Scotland's natural environs is exposed as a naive sentimentalism, an ignorant escape from the "state of affairs" of the Scottish life and its subordination to English culture. The nationalist image of the kilted and broadsword-bearing military masters, of Wallace or MacGregor commandingly wandering the Highlands, is replaced by four skinny underdressed and defeated urban working-class young men sipping cans of warm beer on a chilly gray hill. Tommy's reply is only a "sorry," a realization of the apparent futility of his mission as the four turn back towards home — an indication that the picture of the "servile, pathetic trash" that is Scotland, or at least this part of it, has gained its final victory over the myths of romantic nationalism.

In this diatribe the disturbing assumption that being colonized is a matter of "choice" and that Scotland's major historical flaw has been that it neglected to "pick a decent culture to be colonized by," so corrupts the discourse of colonial relationships that one wonders if correcting its effects are at all possible. That is, Renton's construction not only subverts romantic nationalist images of Scotland with its self-abnegation but also any other political discourse that may attempt to reverse power differences, as if perhaps those too are doomed by an idealist naiveté. When being ruled is seen as an unavoidable matter of choice between one master or another, the only option, it

character, a stark contrast to the fragmented collage of the film's introduction. More importantly, the choices this time around are not disembodied ultimatums of "Choose life," but a personalized plan, presented in the first person, as his own:

> I'm cleaning up and I'm moving on [smiles], going straight and choosing life. I'm looking forward to it already. I'm going to be just like you: the job, the family, the fucking big television, the washing machine, the car, the compact disc and electrical tin opener, good health, low cholesterol, dental insurance, mortgage, starter home ... indexed pension, tax exemption, clearing the gutters, getting by, looking ahead, to the day you die.

With £16,000 in his pocket, the "choices" look much better. The vitriolic condemnation of repeated "fucking" in the opening monologue takes new meaning with the sole enthusiastic "fucking" of a very large television, while the rhymed "pension" and "exemption," "getting by" and "day you die," transform the prose from Renton's opening rant to bouncy verse, casually synched with the bass and high-hat rhythms of the accompanying dance track. Even though Renton's plan takes on a more positive shape, the film does not completely capitulate to the consumer individualist model it invokes. Despite Renton's pledges of transformation, the "choices" still appear hollow and not quite satisfying, "looking ahead until the day you die." But given the conditions Renton is provided, they are offered as the best options, and now they are certainly available to him. His final close-up turns to a fuzzy set of indistinct shades as he walks so far into the camera that it can no longer distinguish the lines of his body — as if we might see right through him. At the same time, the image is all him, too large for the camera, and, it seems, too good to be true. What is nevertheless underscored in the prose and the close-up shot is Renton's control; neither the camera nor the language can keep up with him, as though he is playing a game and staying ahead of the discourse he is entering into — and winning. His autonomy and mobility are ultimately reinforced amidst the quick-paced back-stabbing and self-gratifying chaos of his post–Scottish life.

Like many representations of Scotland, *Trainspotting* is concerned about being British as much as it is about being Scottish. It is a welcome departure not only from cinematic narratives of Scottish quaintness but also from other 1990s English box-office smashes of the period like *Four Weddings and a Funeral* or *The Full Monty* that either extol the London yuppie culture or exploit comic images of an entertaining working class. And its not-quite-certain acceptance of a cynical postmodern player leaves at least some room for a critique of uncomplicated portraits of pleasure and conflict in British culture. What is important to the interpretation of Scottish film and its obviously burgeoning national industry, as well as the Hollywood stranglehold on Scottish history, is that competing images of Scotland are produced from, and directed at, multiple international sites. And with the recent eager cooperation of the Scottish Office to attract American filmmakers like Gibson to Scotland's shores, there is no guarantee even that "home-grown" films will offer more complete depictions of Scotland's past or present.

The critical hope is that filmic narratives get out of the holding pattern that has them trapped in male fantasies of individualist heroism. As Sean Connery's influence demonstrates, this is hardly just a problem of movies but an indication of how powerful the discourses of patriarchy and patronage remain in the popular imagination of the Scottish national home, even though they are in part the product of English and American cultural sensibilities. If anything, the case of cinematic Scotland describes the difficulty of locating international popular culture's "imagined communities" solely within physical territories. The cultural and political allegiances implicit in these texts extend beyond a land's boundaries and have real effects on those marginally represented groups still struggling for the material means to interpret their own experiences. But the well-supported figures of Connery, William Wallace, Rob Roy, and even, to some extent, Renton embody the kind of global allegiances of the dominant that only promise a prosperous nationality to a narrowly defined group of upwardly mobile men.

the outcome in this particular arena, constructions of Scotland's cultural and historical home deserve constant critical attention not only because they are so common and widespread, but because they are often dark fantasies parading as benign expressions of heroism or frivolous sentimentality.

CHAPTER NOTES

Chapter One

1. Fintan O'Toole, "Imagining Scotland," *Granta* 56 (Winter 1996): 67.

2. Although not yet in the practice of using a term like "culture," Arnold's almost interchangeable use in the essay of race, genius, philology, sentiment and poetry ultimately resemble the framework that would become central to his definition of culture in his 1869 *Culture and Anarchy*. See chapter 3 of Robert Young's analysis of Arnold's use of race and culture in *Colonial Desire: Hybridity in Theory, Culture and Race* (London: Routledge, 1995), 55–89.

3. Matthew Arnold, "On the Study of Celtic Literature," in *Lectures and Essays in Criticism*, ed. R.H. Super (Ann Arbor: University of Michigan Press, 1965), 384.

4. Christopher Harvie, *Scotland and Nationalism: Scottish Society and Politics 1707–Present* (London: Routledge, 1998), 70–1.

5. Charles Withers, *Gaelic Scotland: The Transformation of a Culture Region* (London: Routledge, 1988), 155.

6. Homi Bhabha. *The Location of Culture* (London: Routledge, 1994), 142.

7. Benedict Anderson, *Imagined Communities* (London: Verso, 1991), 129.

8. Emily Ann Donaldson, *The Scottish Highland Games in America* (Gretna, LA: Pelican Publishing, 1986), 7.

9. Ann Cvetkovich, *Mixed Feelings: Feminism, Mass Culture, and Victorian Sensationalism* (New Brunswick: Rutgers University Press, 1997), 6.

10. Nira Yuval-Davis, *Gender and Nation* (London: Sage, 1997), 3.

11. Chris Haywood and Mairtin Mac an Ghaill, *Men and Masculinities* (Philadelphia: Open University Press, 2003), 53–4.

12. Anne McClintock, "'No Longer in a Future Heaven': Gender, Race and Nationalism," in *Dangerous Liaisons: Gender, Nation, and Postcolonial Perspectives*, ed. Anne McClintock, Aamir Mufti, and Ellen Shohat (Minneapolis: University of Minnesota Press, 1997), 89.

13. R.W. Connell, *Masculinities* (St. Leonard's: Allen and Unwin, 1995), 44.

14. See chapter two of Lindsay Paterson, *The Autonomy of Modern Scotland* (Edinburgh: Edinburgh University Press, 1994), 10–26.

15. Harvie, 14.

16. Alice Brown, David McCrone, Lindsay Paterson and Paula Surridge, *The Scottish Electorate: The 1997 General Election and Beyond* (New York: St. Martin's, 1999), 5.

17. Brown, 61–2.

18. As quoted in Anne McClintock, *Imperial Leather: Race, Gender and Sexuality in the Colonial Contest* (New York: Routledge, 1995), 350.

19. See the liner notes to Dick Gaughan's *Gaughan* (London: Topic, 1978).

20. *Gaughan*.

21. As quoted in Harvie, 204.

22. As quoted in Peter Kravitz's introduction to *The Vintage Book of Contemporary Scottish Fiction* (New York: Random House, 1997), xxxv.

23. Harvie, 215.

24. See Harvie, *Scotland and Nationalism*; S.G.E. Lythe and John Butt, *An Economic History of Scotland* (1975); David McCrone (ed.), *The Making of Scotland: Nation, Culture and Social Change* (1989); Michael Hechter, *Internal Colonialism: The Celtic Fringe in British National Development* (1975); and H.J. Hanham, *Scottish Nationalism* (1969), to name but a few.

25. As quoted in Kravitz, xxii.

26. Tom Leonard, *Six Glasgow Poems* (Glasgow: Midnight Press, 1969).

27. Michael Hardt and Antonio Negri,

Empire (Cambridge: Harvard University Press, 2000), 109.

28. E. San Juan Jr., *Racism and Cultural Studies* (Durham: Duke University Press, 2001), 66.

29. Neil Lazaras, *Nationalism and Cultural Practice in the Postcolonial World* (Cambridge: Cambridge University Press, 1999), 77–78.

30. Benedict Anderson, *Imagined Communities* (London: Verso, 1991), 5.

31. Aijaz Ahmad, *In Theory: Classes, Nations, Literatures* (New York: Verso, 1992), 11.

32. See Chapter Three of David McCrone's *Understanding Scotland: The Sociology of a Stateless Nation* (London: Routledge, 1992) where he asks in the title, "Is Scotland Different?"

33. Theodore Allen, *The Invention of the White Race,* vol. 1: *Racial Oppression and Social Control* (London: Verso, 1994), 72.

34. Ama Ata Aidoo, *Our Sister Killjoy* (White Plains, NY: Longman African Series, 1999), 91–2.

35. Anne McClintock, *Imperial Leather: Race, Gender and Sexuality in the Colonial Contest* (New York: Routledge, 1995), 208–231.

36. Charles Taylor, *Sources of the Self: The Making of Modern Identity* (Cambridge: Cambridge University Press, 1989), 375–6.

37. Arthur Herman, *How the Scots Invented the Modern World: The True Story of How Western Europe's Poorest Nation Created Our World and Everything in It* (New York: Crown, 2001), 361.

38. Herman 301.

Chapter Two

1. Alan Bold, *Modern Scottish Literature* (London: Longman, 1983), 105.

2. Hugh MacDiarmid, *A Drunk Man Looks at the Thistle*, ed. Kenneth Buthlay (Edinburgh: Scottish Academic Press, 1987), 60.

3. Alan Bold, *MacDiarmid: The Terrible Crystal* (London: Routledge, 1983), 55.

4. George Blake, *Barrie and the Kailyard School* (London: Arthur Baker 1951), 51.

5. Blake, 13.

6. It is important to note that there was not an absolute consensus amongst contemporary critics on whether or not Kailyard fiction counted as legitimate high art. Influential reviewer W.E. Henley wrote in the *National Observer* that James Barrie's 1891 novel *The Little Minister* was "what cannot fail to prove the novel

of the year: a year, be it remarked, that has witnessed the production of work by such men as George Meredith [*One of Our Conquerors*], Thomas Hardy [*Tess of the D'Urbervilles*], and Rudyard Kipling [*The Light that Failed*]" (quoted in Whigham Price, "W. Roberston Nicoll and the Genesis of the Kailyard School," *Durham University Journal*, 86.55 [January 1994]: 81). The first few decades of twentieth-century criticism brought with it a significantly more unified voice against the aesthetic value of Kailyard texts.

7. For a history of Nicoll's publishing activity with Kailyard authors in his journal the *British Weekly*, see Price, 79.

8. Blake, 40.

9. Islay Murray Donaldson, "Crockett and the Fabric of *The Lilac Sunbonnet*," *Studies in Scottish Fiction: Nineteenth Century,* ed. Horst Drescher and Joachim Schwend (New York: Verlag Peter Lang, 1985), 305.

10. See Thomas Knowles, *Ideology, Art and Commerce* (Goteborg, Sweden: Acta Universitatis Gothoburgensis, 1983), 23.

11. Mary Poovey writes in *Uneven Developments: The Ideological Work of Gender in Mid-Victorian England* (Chicago: University of Chicago Press, 1988): "I give the phrase ideological work two different emphases. In one sense, it means the 'work of ideology': representations of gender at mid-century were part of a system of interdependent images in which various ideologies became accessible to individual men and women. In another sense, however, the phrase means 'the work of making ideology': representations of gender constituted one of the sites on which ideological systems were simultaneously constructed and contested..." [2].

12. Benedict Anderson defines nation in *Imagined Communities* (London: Verso, 1991), "I propose the following definition of nation: it is an imagined political community — and imagined as both inherently limited and sovereign" (5–6).

13. A significant part of this argument is borrowed from Anne McClintock's *Imperial Leather: Race, Gender and Sexuality in the Colonial Contest* (New York: Routledge, 1995), a compelling analysis of nineteenth-century colonialism and narratives of domestic harmony. Her central argument is that the ideas of Victorian domesticity in Britain and in the colonies became suffused with the colonial ideas of race; "as domestic space became racialized, colonial space became domesticated" (36).

14. Ian Maclaren, *Beside the Bonnie Brier Bush* (New York: Hurst and Co., 1896), 7. Here-

after cited parenthetically in the text and abbreviated *BBB*.

15. Edwin Muir, *Scott and Scotland: The Predicament of the Scottish Writer* (New York: Speller, 1938), 160–161.

16. Eric Anderson, "The Kailyard Revisited," *Nineteenth Century Scottish Fiction,* ed. Ian Campbell (New York: Barnes and Noble, 1979), 146.

17. Katie Trumpener, "National Character, Nationalist Plots: National Tale and Historical Novel in the Age of Waverley, 1806–1830," *ELH* 60 (1993): 685.

18. See Ina Ferris, *The Achievement of Literary Authority: Gender, History and the Waverley Novels* (Ithaca: Cornell University Press, 1991), especially chapter four, "From 'National Tale' to 'Historical Novel'" (105–133), which outlines the generic relationship of Scott's fiction — and its history of consumption — to the novels of Maria Edgeworth and Lady Morgan. Ian Duncan's *Modern Romance and the Transformation of the Novel* (London: Cambridge University Press, 1992) shrewdly demonstrates that Scott's Waverley novels incorporate details of historical conflict as a means to effectively close their collective import in favor of a retranslated sentimentality that valorizes a historically situated, but private and politically removed middle-class individual: "[T]he Waverley novels discover history in order to discover the horizon at which — as for the individual subject, so for the nation — history comes to a stop" (53). My concern here is the conventional comparison of Kailyard fiction to the Waverley novels rather than the entirety of Scott's rich oeuvre.

19. Tom Nairn, *The Break-Up of Britain: Crisis and Neo-Nationalism* (London: NLB, 1977), 98.

20. Homi Bhabha, *The Location of Culture* (London: Routledge, 1994), 142.

21. Raymond Williams, *The Country and the City* (New York: Oxford University Press, 1973), 120.

22. See Charles Withers, "Class, Culture and Migrant Identity: Gaelic Highlanders in Urban Scotland," in *Urbanizing Britain: Essays on Class and Community in the Nineteenth Century,* ed. Charles Withers and Gerry Kearns (Cambridge: Cambridge University Press, 1991), 55–79, for an analysis of Highland population and migration in nineteenth-century Scottish cities.

23. As quoted in J.A.D. Blaikie, "The Country and the City: Sexuality and social class in Victorian Scotland," in *Urbanizing Britain: Essays on Class and Community in the Nineteenth Century,* ed. Charles Withers and Gerry Kearns (Cambridge: Cambridge University Press, 1991), 95.

24. James Barrie, *The Little Minister* (New York: Russel, 1898), 14. Hereafter cited parenthetically in the text and abbreviated *TLM*.

25. James Barrie, *Auld Licht Idylls* (New York: Scribners, 1906), 11. Hereafter cited parenthetically in the text and abbreviated *ALI*.

26. S.R. Crockett, *The Stickit Minister* (London: MacMillan, 1893), 146–7. Hereafter cited parenthetically in the text and abbreviated *TSM*.

27. According to census data of 1891 over a quarter of a million people throughout Scotland (6.3%) spoke Gaelic, of which 40,000 spoke Gaelic only. The percentages of Gaelic speakers in the Highlands were substantially higher. Charles Withers has shown in *Gaelic in Scotland: The Geographical History of a Language* (Edinburgh: John Donald Publishers, 1984) that this translated to almost 18,000 speakers in Glasgow and between 50–80 percent of Highland inhabitants still speaking Gaelic as their primary language.

28. B. Anderson, 44.

29. As quoted in page three of the back advertisement of the MacMillan's 1894 American fifth edition of Crockett's *The Stickit Minister and Some Common Men.*

30. See the review of Barrie's *Margaret Ogilvy* in *Blackwoods Edinburgh Journal* 162 (April 1897): 481–483.

31. See John McInnes's preface to the 1992 reprint of Alexander Carmichael's *Carmina Gadelica: Charms of the Gaels* (Edinburgh: Lindisfarne Press), 1–18.

32. William Skene lays out his dissatisfaction with previous Scottish historians in the first chapter of vol. 1, "History and Ethnology," in *Celtic Scotland: A History of Ancient Alban* (Edinburgh: Edmonston & Douglas, 1876), 1–28.

33. Celtic history in general, whether Irish, Welsh or Scottish, gained popularity at the end of the nineteenth century. The 1896 *Lyra Celtica,* for example (Edinburgh: Patrick Geddes, 1896), edited by Elizabeth Sharp, describes itself as a pan-national Celtic poetic archive: "[A]n effort is made to illustrate the distinguishing imaginative qualities of the several Celtic races; to trace the origins, dispersion, interfusion, and concentration of the early Celtic, Picto-Celtic, and later Goidelic and Brythonic peoples, and to reflect Celtic mythopoeic and authentic history through Celtic poetry and legendary lore. Concurrently there is an endeavor to relate, in nat-

ural order, the development of the literature of contemporary Wales, Brittany, Ireland, and Celtic Scotland, from their ancient Cymric, Armorican, Erse, and Alban-Gaelic congeners" [xx].

34. Caroline Bingham, *Beyond the Highland Line* (London: Constable, 1991), 188.

35. Simon Fraser, *The Airs and Melodies Peculiar to the Highlands of Scotland and the Isles* (Inverness: Logan & Co., 1874). The renewed interest in Scottish Gaelic poetry in the 1870s and 1880s also led to the increased publication of numerous collections, including the initiation of the 1880 journal *The Celtic Review*, Archibald Sinclair's *Ant' Oranaiche, or the Gaelic Songster* (1879), Ernest Renan's *Poetry of the Celtic Races* (1884), J.F. Campbell's *Leabhar Na Feinne, Heroic Gaelic Ballads Collected in Scotland* (1872), and John Blackie's *The Language and Literature of the Scottish Highlands* (1876). Many others followed in the next century, including *Literature of the Highlands* by Magnus Maclean in 1903, John Mackenzie's 1907 *Beauties of Gaelic Poetry and the Lives of the Highland Bards*, and Dougald Mitchell's *Book of Highland Verse* (1912), to name only a few. Scotland's North and West regions were regarded as a wellspring of knowledge to be seized, and even extended to horticultural studies like Murdoch McNeill's *Colosnay, One of the Hebrides: Its Plants, Their Local Names and Uses*. And this knowledge took on the institutional form of the Chair of Celtic Studies founded in 1882 at the University of Edinburgh, a position still held by distinguished Gaelic scholars. In 1891 An Comunn Gaidehealach (The Highland Association) assembled for the first time and soon established the national "Mod," a competitive festival of Gaelic speech, literature, and vocal and instrumental music (see Bingham 191).

36. The first volume, *Fragments of Ancient Poetry, collected in the Highlands of Scotland, and translated from the Gaelic or Erse Language*, was released in 1760, followed by *Fingal* (1761) and *Temora* (1763).

37. See Malcolm Chapman, *The Gaelic Vision in Scottish Culture* (London, 1978), 37–64, Robert Crawford, *Devolving English Literature* (Oxford: Oxford University Press, 1992), and Katie Trumpener, *Bardic Nationalism* (Princeton: Princeton University Press, 1997), for more on Ossian's impact in Europe and Scottish national identity.

38. Hugh Trevor-Roper, "The Invention of Tradition: The Highland Tradition of Scotland," in *The Invention of Tradition*, ed. Eric Hobs-

bawm and Terence Ranger (Cambridge: Cambridge University Press), 12–42.

39. See T.C. Smout, "Tours in the Scottish Highlands from Eighteenth to the Twentieth Centuries" in *Northern Scotland* 5, 2 (1983): 99–122. The investiture of "relief" roads and extended railways into the Highlands, as well the Game Act of 1831, which encouraged the growth of "Deer Forest" acreage for wealthy sport hunters, helped to create what Smout calls the "vulgar tourism" of the 1800s.

40. Charles Withers, *Gaelic Scotland: The Transformation of a Culture Region* (London: Routledge: 1988). See especially chapter II, "Civilization and the Move to Improvement," 57–109.

41. Alexander Carmichael, *Carmina Gadelica: Charms of the Gaels* (Edinburgh: Lindisfarne Press, 1992), 24. Hereafter cited parenthetically in the text and abbreviated *CG*.

42. The *Waifs and Strays* series included five individually published volumes of *Craignish Tales, Folk and Hero Tales* (in two volumes), *The Fians; or Stories, Poems, and Traditions of Fionn and His Warrior Band*, and *Clan Traditions and Popular Tales of the Western Highlands and Islands*.

43. John Gregorson Campbell and Alfred Nutt, eds., *Clan Traditions and Popular Tales of the Western Highlands and Islands* (London: David Nutt, 1895), 501.

44. D. McInnes, "Introduction" to his edited collection, *Folk and Hero Tales* (London: Folk-Lore Society, 1890), ix-x.

45. Matthew Arnold, "On the Study of Celtic Literature," in *Lectures and Essays in Criticism*, ed. R.H. Super (Ann Arbor: University of Michigan Press, 1965), 384. Hereafter cited parenthetically in the text and abbreviated *L*.

46. Robert Young, *Colonial Desire: Hybridity in Theory, Culture and Race* (London: Routledge, 1995), 70–1.

47. Young, 71–2.

48. Alfred Nutt, "Introduction" to *Clan Traditions and Popular Tales*, vol. 5 of *The Waifs and Strays of the Celtic Tradition* (London: David Nutt, 1895), xvi.

49. Nutt, xvi.

50. See McClintock on the genealogical time in the "family" of race, 38–9.

51. Nutt, xii.

52. Price attributes this quote to Nicoll's successor editor, J.M.E., 75.

53. Price, 70.

54. E.P. Thompson illustrates in his *The Making of the English Working Class* (New York: Vintage, 1963) that new forms of production, especially between 1790 and 1850, were widely

seen as emblems of the new industrial way of life: "[S]team power and the cotton-mill = new working class. The physical instruments of production were seen as giving rise in a direct and more-or-less compulsive way to new social relationships, institutions and cultural modes" (191).

55. T.M. Devine argues that while there was substantial discrimination against Highlanders in the city, Highlanders were easier to assimilate because of common ties to religion and ethnicity with Lowland Scots: "Highland migration was never as significant in numerical terms as the Irish movement and contemporary observers regarded the increasing waves of Irish immigrants as an alarming threat to jobs, health, civilization and the Protestant religion itself. But the Highlanders were more easily absorbed." See *Clanship to Crofters' War: The Social Transformation of the Scottish Highlands* (Manchester: Manchester University Press, 1994), 248.

56. McClintock's *Imperial Leather* argues that the nineteenth century saw a shift from scientific racism to commodity racism whereupon domestic cleanliness was heavily imbued with metaphors of national "whitening" and purification. See especially chapter five, "Soft-soaping Empire" (208–231).

57. B. Anderson, 64.

58. See the review of Barrie's *Sentimental Tommy* in *Blackwoods Edinburgh Journal* 162 (Dec 1896): 800–813.

59. T.W.H. Crosland, *The Unspeakable Scot* (London: Grant Richards, 1902), 78.

60. Quoted in Bold, *Modern Scottish Literature*, 107.

61. My argument owes much to Ann Cvetkovich's second chapter, "Theorizing Affect," in *Mixed Feelings: Feminism, Mass Culture, and Victorian Sensationalism* (New Brunswick: Rutgers, 1992), where she argues: "If affect is historically constructed, it can then become, as Foucault suggests of sexuality under the rule of repressive hypothesis, not the mechanism for the liberation of the self but instead the mechanism for containment and discipline of the self" (31).

62. Ernest Gellner, *Thought and Change* (London: Weidenfeld and Nicholson, 1964), 169.

63. Quoted in Saree Makdisi's study of Walter Scott's *Waverley*, "Colonial Space and the Colonization of Time in Scott's Waverley," *Studies in Romanticism* 34 (Summer 1995): 155–187. Makdisi provides a brief history of eighteenth- and nineteenth-century enclosure policy in the Scottish Highlands.

64. Quoted in Richard Rodger, "Employment, Wages and Poverty in the Scottish Cities," *Per-*

spectives of the Scottish City, ed. George Gordon (Aberdeen: Aberdeen University Press, 1985), 27.

65. Elaine Showalter, *Sexual Anarchy: Gender and Culture at the Fin de Siècle* (New York: Viking, 1990), 9.

66. As quoted from the "Reports of the Select Committee on the Contagious Diseases Act" (1881) in Linda Mahood, "The Domestication of 'Fallen' Women: The Glasgow Magdalene Institution, 1860–1890" in *The Magdalenes: Prostitution in the Nineteenth Century* (New York: Routledge, 1990), (146–7). Mahood's history of urban Scotland's efforts to expand its apparatuses of social control locally situates the trends throughout the British Empire to "rehabilitate" and discipline poor and disenfranchised women. She argues that in an effort to "save" women, institutions were formed around the category of "Magdalenes," "newly fallen daughters of pious parents" who had a minimal history of offenses but were not yet considered "criminal." Successful rehabilitation and moral restoration still meant the return of these women to middle-class domestic settings: marrying, or remaining with relatives, or placement in domestic service. Many "unreformed" women left these institutions to become factory workers or self-employed tradeswomen, while others resisted the bourgeois moral code altogether by ignoring it, resisting it, or leaving the Institution permanently (158).

67. See Blaikie, 95.

68. McClintock, 354–5. See also Nira Yuval-Davis and Floya Anthias, *Women-Nation-State* (London: Macmillan, 1989) on the five ways that women have been figured in nationalism:

— as biological reproducers of the members of national collectivities
— as reproducers of the boundaries of national groups (through restrictions on sexual or marital relations)
— as active transmitters and producers of the national culture
— as symbolic signifiers of national difference
— as active participants in national struggles [354–5].

69. McClintock, 363.

70. McClintock, 359.

Chapter Three

1. Edwin Muir, *Scott and Scotland: The Predicament of the Scottish Writer* (New York:

Speller, 1938). Hereafter citations will appear parenthetically in the text.

2. As quoted in James Veitch's critical biography, *George Douglas Brown* (London: Herbert Jenkins, 1952), 153.

3. There are certainly more inclusive versions of the Scottish Renaissance. Many successful works were produced by authors like Rebecca West, Nan Sheperd, Kate Karswell, and Naomi Mitchison at the time as well. My purpose here is to address the terms in which the Scottish Renaissance, as a historical category in the first half of the twentieth century, developed its canonical reputation. The critical reevaluation of the Scottish Renaissance in the 1980s and later by such scholars as Glenda Norquay and Carol Anderson illustrate that most contemporary and later discussions of the movement omit the active personal and literary relationships between widely read women writers and the male writers recognized as members of the Scottish Renaissance. See Anderson and Norquay, "Superiorism," *Cencrastus* 15 (1984): 8–10, Carol Anderson and Aileen Christianson, *Scottish Women's Fiction, 1920s to 1960s: Journeys into Being* (East Linton: Tuckwell, 2000) and *A History of Scottish Women's Writing*, ed. Douglas Gifford and Dorothy McMillan (Edinburgh: Edinburgh University Press, 1997).

4. See Christopher Harvie, *Scotland and Nationalism: Scottish Society and Politics 1707 to the Present* (London: Routledge, 1998), 26.

5. As quoted in Harvie, 74.

6. Frank Gloversmith, ed., *Class Culture and Social Change: A New View of the 1930's* (Sussex: Harvester Press, 1980).

7. Benedict Anderson, *Imagined Communities* (London: Verso, 1991), 133.

8. T.S. Eliot's "The Social Function of Poetry," in *On Poetry and Poets* (London: Faber and Faber, 1957), 21.

9. See Duncan Glen, *Hugh MacDiarmid and the Scottish Renaissance* (Edinburgh: W. & R. Chambers, 1964), 106–108.

10. See Maurice Lindsay's introduction to the 1976 edition of *Modern Scottish Poetry: An Anthology of the Scottish Renaissance* (Manchester: Carcanet Press, 1976), 18.

11. See Robert Crawford, *Devolving English Literature* (Oxford: Oxford University Press, 1992), especially chapter 2, "British Literature" (45–110), for the historical beginnings of the Anglicization of Scottish literature.

12. See Henry Louis Gates Jr., *Loose Canons: Notes on the Culture Wars* (New York: Oxford University Press, 1992), especially chapter 2,

"The Master's Pieces: On Canon Formation and the African-American Tradition," 17–42.

13. MacDiarmid later published works with an eye on the history of Scottish culture, such as his edited poetry collections *Robert Burns* (1926), *The Golden Treasury of Scottish Poetry* (1940), and *Selections from the Poems of William Dunbar* (1952).

14. As quoted in Glen, 74–75.

15. Burger's use of the term "historical avant-garde" identifies a historical division between pre- and post–World War II experimental art and literature. See Peter Burger's *Theory of the Avant-Garde* (Minneapolis: University of Minnesota Press, 1988), which describes the historical avant-garde's challenge to the practices of "institution art" as unprecedented and unreplicated. After the failure (in Burger's view) of the historical avant-garde, after its critique of bourgeois cultural styles was recuperated by the institutions it attacked, critical art following the practices established by the historical avant-garde is better understood (for Burger as for others) as "neo-avant-garde," as belonging to a different period shaped by different conflicts and concerns.

16. Mikhail Bakhtin, *The Dialogic Imagination*, ed. Michael Holquist (Austin: University of Texas Press, 1981), 13.

17. Bakhtin, 17.

18. See Tony Crowley, *The Politics of Discourse* (London: Routledge, 1989).

19. Hereafter, all references to *A Drunk Man Looks at the Thistle* will be cited by page from *Hugh MacDiarmid: The Complete Poems*, vol. I (London: Carcanet Press Limited, 1993).

20. As quoted in Catherin Kerrigan's *Whaur Extremes Meet: The Poetry of Hugh MacDiarmid* (Edinburgh: The Mercat Press, 1983), 60.

21. Rena Grant, "Synthetic Scots: Hugh MacDiarmid's Imagined Community," in *Hugh MacDiarmid: Man and Poet*, ed. Nancy Gish (Orono: National Poetry Foundation, 1992), 200.

22. Hugh MacDiarmid, *Lucky Poet* (Berkeley: University of California Press, 1972), 404.

23. Anderson, 6.

24. Grant, 199.

25. See chapter 1 "Varieties of Scots" in John Corbett's *Language and Scottish Literature* (Edinburgh: Edinburgh University Press, 1998), 1–21.

26. Mary Louise Pratt, "Linguistic Utopias" in *The Linguistics of Writing: Arguments Between Language and Literature*, ed. Nigel Fabb, Derek Attridge, Alan Durant, and Colin MacCabe (New York: Methuen Inc., 1987), 56.

27. Pratt, 51.

28. MacDiarmid, *Lucky Poet*, 141–2.

land Games in America. Gretna, LA: Pelican Publishing, 1986.

Donaldson, Islay Murray. "Crockett and the Fabric of *The Lilac Sunbonnet*." In *Studies in Scottish Fiction: Nineteenth Century*. Ed. Horst Drescher and Joachim Schwend. New York: Verlag Peter Lang, 1985.

Duncan, Ian. *Modern Romance and the Transformation of the Novel*. London: Cambridge University Press, 1992.

Eliot, T.S. "The Social Function of Poetry." In *On Poetry and Poets*. London: Faber and Faber, 1957.

Enloe, Cynthia. *Maneuvers: The International Politics of Militarizing Women's Lives*. Berkeley: University of California Press, 2000.

Ferris, Ina. *The Achievement of Literary Authority: Gender, History and the Waverley Novels*. Ithaca: Cornell University Press, 1991.

Fraser, Douglas. "Connery Denied Knighthood Over Scots Nationalist Links." *Sunday Times*, February 22, 1998.

Fraser, Douglas, and Ian Hernon. "The Scottish Office Presents Dr. No." *Sunday Times*. 1 March 1998. http://www.Sunday-Times.co.uk/.

Fraser, Simon. *The Airs and Melodies Peculiar to the Highlands of Scotland and the Isles*. Inverness: Logan & Co., 1874.

Gates, Henry Louis. *Loose Canons: Notes on the Culture Wars*. New York: Oxford University Press, 1992.

Gaughan, Dick. *Gaughan*. London: Topic, 1978.

Gellner, Ernest. *Thought and Change*. London: Weidenfeld and Nicholson, 1964.

Gibbon, Lewis Grassic. *A Scots Quair*. London: Pan Books, 1982.

Gifford, Douglas, and Dorothy McMillan, eds. *A History of Scottish Women's Writing*. Edinburgh: Edinburgh University Press, 1997.

Gilroy, Paul. *There Ain't No Black in the Union Jack: The Cultural Politics of Race and Nation*. Chicago: University of Chicago Press, 1987.

Gish, Nancy. "MacDiarmid Reading the Wasteland: The Politics of Quotation." In *Hugh MacDiarmid: Man and Poet*. Ed. Nancy Gish. Orono: National Poetry Foundation, 1992.

Glen, Duncan. *Hugh MacDiarmid and the Scottish Renaissance*. Edinburgh: W. & R. Chambers, 1964.

Gloversmith, Frank, ed. *Class Culture and Social Change: A New View of the 1930's*. New Jersey: Humanities Press, 1980.

Grant, Rena. "Synthetic Scots: Hugh MacDiarmid's Imagined Community." In *Hugh MacDiarmid: Man and Poet*. Ed. Nancy Gish. Orono: National Poetry Foundation, 1992.

Grieve, Michael, and W.R. Aitken, eds. *Hugh MacDiarmid: The Complete Poems*, Vol. I (London: Carcanet Press Limited, 1993).

Gunn, Neil. *Highland River*. London: Hutchison, 1974.

Hague, Euan. "National Tartan Day: Rewriting History in the United States." *Scottish Affairs* 38 (Winter 2002): 94–124.

_____. "Texts as Flags: The League of the South and the development of nationalist intelligentsia in the United States 1975–2001." *HAGAR: International Social Science Review* 3, 2 (2002): 299–339.

Hall, Stuart. "The Meaning of New Times." In *Critical Dialogues in Cultural Studies*. Eds. David Morely and Kuan-Hsing Chen. London: Routledge, 1996.

_____. "New Ethnicities." In *Critical Dialogues in Cultural Studies*. Eds. David Morely and Kuan-Hsing Chen. London: Routledge, 1996.

Halter, Marilyn. *Shopping for Identity: the Marketing of Ethnicity*. New York: Schocken Books, 2000.

Handler, Richard, and Jocelyn Linnekin. "Tradition, Genuine or Spurious." *Journal of American Folklore* 97 (1984): 193–210.

Hanham, H.J. *Scottish Nationalism*. London: Faber and Faber, 1969.

Hardt, Michael, and Antonio Negri. *Empire*. Cambridge: Harvard University Press, 2000.

Harvie, Christopher. *Scotland and Nationalism: Scottish Society and Politics 1707-Present.* London: Routledge, 1998.

Haywood, Chris, and Mairtin Mac an Ghaill. *Men and Masculinities.* Philadelphia: Open University Press, 2003.

Hechter, Michael. *Internal Colonialism: The Celtic Fringe in British National Development.* London: Routledge & Kegan Paul, 1975.

Herman, Arthur. *How the Scots Invented the Modern World: The True Story of How Western Europe's Poorest Nation Created Our World and Everything in It.* New York: Crown, 2001.

Hewison, Robert. "Commerce and Culture." In *Enterprise and Heritage: Crosscurrents of National Culture.* Eds. John Corner and Sylvia Harvey. New York: Routledge, 1991.

_____. *The Heritage Industry: Britain in a Climate of Decline.* London: Methuen, 1987.

_____. "Heritage Interpretation." In *Heritage Interpretation: The Natural and Built Environment.* Ed. David Uzell. London: Belhaven Press, 1989.

Hornblower, Margaret. "Roots Mania." *Time* 153, 15 (April 19, 1999): 54–63.

Huyssen. Andreas. *After the Great Divide: Modernism, Mass Culture, Postmodernism.* Bloomington: Indiana University Press, 1986.

Jacobson, Matthew Frye. *Whiteness of a Different Color: Immigration and the Alchemy of Race.* Cambridge, MA: Harvard University Press, 1998.

Jameson, Fredric. *Postmodernism or the Cultural Logic of Late Capitalism.* Durham: Duke University Press, 1991.

Jarvie, Grant. *The Highland Games: The Making of the Myth.* Edinburgh: Edinburgh University Press, 1991.

Jeffords, Susan. *Hard Bodies: Hollywood Masculinity in the Reagan Era.* New Brunswick: Rutgers University Press, 1994.

Jeffries, Bruce. "Come South to the Highlands!" *The Armstrong Chronicles* 17, 1–2 (Spring/Summer 1998).

Kaplan, Cora. "Millennial Class." *PMLA* 115: 1 (January, 2000): 9–19.

Kerrigan, Catherin. *Whaur Extremes Meet: The Poetry of Hugh MacDiarmid.* Edinburgh: The Mercat Press, 1983.

Klein, Naomi. *No Logo.* New York: Penguin, 2000.

Knowles, Thomas. *Ideology, Art and Commerce.* Goteborg, Sweden: Acta Universitatis Gothoburgensis, 1983.

Kravitz, Peter, ed. *The Vintage Book of Contemporary Scottish Fiction.* New York: Random House, 1997.

Lang, Stuart. "Presenting 'Things as they are': John Sommerfield's *May Day* and Mass Observation." In *Class Culture and Social Change: A New View of the 1930's.* Ed. Frank Gloversmith. Sussex: Harvester Press, 1980.

Lawrence, Pam. "Hunky Men in Kilts. *Monarch of the Glen*'s popularity continues." 5 September 2007. http://www.belaonline.com/articles/art44345.asp.

Lazaras, Neil. *Nationalism and Cultural Practice in the Postcolonial World.* Cambridge: Cambridge University Press, 1999.

Leonard, Tom. *Six Glasgow Poems.* Glasgow: Midnight Press, 1969.

Lindsay, Maurice, ed. *Modern Scottish Poetry: An Anthology of the Scottish Renaissance.* Manchester: Carcanet Press, 1976.

Lodge, David. *Ireland After History.* South Bend: Notre Dame University Press, 2000.

Lowenthal, David. *The Heritage Crusade and the Spoils of History.* Cambridge: Cambridge University Press, 1998.

Lukacs, Georg. "The Novels of Willi Bredel." In *Essays on Realism.* Ed. Rodney Livingstone. Trans. David Fernbach. Cambridge: MIT Press, 1981.

Lythe, S.G.E., and John Butt. *An Economic History of Scotland.* Glasgow: Blackie & Son Ltd., 1975.

MacDiarmid, Hugh. *A Drunk Man Looks at the Thistle.* Ed. Kenneth Buthlay. Edinburgh: Scottish Academic Press, 1987.

_____. *Albyn; or Scotland and the Future.* London: Kegan Paul, 1927.

_____. *Lucky Poet*. Berkeley: University of California Press, 1972.

Maclaren, Ian. *Beside the Bonnie Brier Bush*. New York: Hurst and Co., 1896.

Macmillan, David S. "Scottish Enterprise and Influences in Canada, 1620–1900." In *The Scots Abroad*. Ed. R.A. Cage. Kent: Croom Helm, 1985.

Mahood, Linda. *The Magdalenes: Prostitution in the Nineteenth Century*. New York: Routledge, 1990.

Makdisi, Saree. "Colonial Space and the Colonization of Time in Scott's *Waverley*." *Studies in Romanticism* 34 (Summer 1995): 155–187.

Marcus, Greil. *Lipstick Traces: A Secret History of the 20th Century*. Cambridge, MA: Harvard University Press, 1989.

"*Margaret Ogilvy*." *Blackwoods Edinburgh Journal* 162 (April 1897): 481–483.

Martin, Joel. *Sacred Revolt: The Muskogees' Struggle for a New World*. Boston: Beacon Press, 1991.

McArthur, Colin. *Brigadoon, Braveheart and the Scots: Distortions of Scotland in Hollywood Cinema*. London: I.B. Tauris, 2003.

McClintock, Anne. *Imperial Leather: Race, Gender and Sexuality in the Colonial Contest*. New York: Routledge, 1996.

_____. "'No Longer in a Future Heaven': Gender, Race and Nationalism." In *Dangerous Liaisons: Gender, Nation, and Postcolonial Perspectives*. Eds. Anne McClintock, Aamir Mufti, and Ellen Shohat. Minneapolis: University of Minnesota Press, 1997.

McCrone, David, ed. *The Making of Scotland: Nation, Culture and Social Change*. Edinburgh: Edinburgh University Press, 1989.

_____. *Understanding Scotland: The Sociology of a Stateless Nation*. London: Routledge, 1992.

McCrone, David, Angela Morris, and Richard Kiely. *Scotland—The Brand: The Making of Scottish Heritage*. Edinburgh: Polygon, 1995.

McInnes, D., ed. *Folk and Hero Tales*. London: Folk-Lore Society, 1890.

Mies, Maria. *Patriarchy and Accumulation on a World Scale: Women in the International Division of Labor*. London: Zed Books, 1986.

Muir, Edwin. *Scott and Scotland: The Predicament of the Scottish Writer*. New York: Speller, 1938.

Nairn, Tom. *The Break-Up of Britain: Crisis and Neo-Nationalism*. London: New Left Books, 1977.

_____. "Gordon Brown: a Pastor Takes Power." 26 June 2007. http://scottishfutures.typepad.com/scottish_futures/2007/06/the-nairnospher.html.

The National Trust for Scotland: Visit Scotland's Best. Advertising pamphlet, 1998.

O'Toole, Fintan. "Imagining Scotland." *Granta* 56 (Winter 1996): 59–76.

Paterson, Lindsay. *The Autonomy of Modern Scotland*. Edinburgh: Edinburgh University Press, 1994.

Pittock, Murray. *The Invention of Scotland: The Stuart Myth and Scottish Identity, 1638-Present*. London: Routledge, 1991.

_____. *The Myth of the Jacobite Clans*. Edinburgh: Edinburgh University Press, 1995.

Poovey, Mary. *Uneven Developments: The Ideological Work of Gender in Mid-Victorian England*. Chicago: University of Chicago Press, 1988.

Prashad, Vijay. *The Karma of Brown Folk*. Minneapolis: Minnesota University Press, 2000.

Pratt, Mary Louise. *Imperial Eyes: Travel Writing and Transculturation*. London: Routledge, 1992.

_____. "Linguistic Utopias." In *The Linguistics of Writing: Arguments Between Language and Literature*. Eds. Nigel Fabb et al. New York: Methuen Inc., 1987.

Prebble, John. *The Highland Clearances*. London: Secker and Warburg, 1963.

Price, Whigham. "W. Roberston Nicoll and the Genesis of the Kailyard School." *Durham University Journal* 86.55 (January 1994): 73–82.

Ritchie, Murray. "Labor's Nightmare Scenario." *The Glasgow Herald*. 10 March

1998. http://www.wp.com/ Alba/opinion poll.html.

Ritchie, Murray, Ken Smith, and Alexander Linklater. "A Nation Again by Year 2013." *The Glasgow Herald.* 30 March 1997. http://www.wp.com/Alba/mori.html.

Ritchie, Murray, and Robbie Dinwoodie. "SNP Surge Stuns Labor." *The Glasgow Herald.* 10 March 1998. http://www.wp.com/Alba/opinionpoll.html.

Rodger, Richard. "Employment, Wages and Poverty in the Scottish Cities." In *Perspectives of the Scottish City.* Ed. George Gordon. Aberdeen: Aberdeen University Press, 1985.

Roquemore, Joseph. *History Goes to the Movies.* New York: Main Street Books, 1999.

Rosie, George. "Museumry and the Heritage Industry." In *The Manufacture of Scottish History.* Eds. Ian Donnachie and Christopher Watley. Edinburgh: Polygon, 1992.

Said, Edward. *Culture and Imperialism.* New York: Knopf, 1993.

San Juan Jr., E. *Racism and Cultural Studies.* Durham: Duke University Press, 2001.

Schuffert, Joy. "Don and Joy Schuffert's Scotland Trip. *Bell-A-Peal: Official Publication of the Bell Family Association of the United States* 12.2 (Spring 1998): 3.

Scott, Alexander, and Douglas Gifford, eds. *Neil M. Gunn: The Man and the Writer.* Edinburgh: William Blackwood, 1973.

Scott, Gill, and Gerry Mooney. "Devolution, deprivation and disadvantage: lessons from Scotland." *Poverty* 126 (Winter 2007): 12–14.

Scott, Joan Wallach. *Gender and the Politics of History.* New York: Columbia, 1988.

The Scottish Coalition. "Celebrate Tartan Day." Advertisement. *Scottish Life* 4, 2 (Spring 1999): 19.

Scottish Executive. "Social Justice: a Scotland where everyone matters." 1999. http://www.scotland.gov.uk.

Scottish National Party. "Putting Scottish Film in the Picture: A Consultative Paper on the Scottish Film Industry." 10 March 1996. http://www.snp.org/uk/library/rr96050a.html.

"*Sentimental Tommy.*" *Blackwoods Edinburgh Journal* 162 (Dec 1896): 800–813.

Sharp, Elizabeth, ed. *Lyra Celtica.* Edinburgh: Patrick Geddes, 1896.

Showalter, Elaine. *Sexual Anarchy: Gender and Culture at the Fin de Siècle.* New York: Viking, 1990.

Skene, William. *Celtic Scotland: A History of Ancient Alban.* Edinburgh: Edmonston & Douglas, 1876.

Smout, T.C. "Tours in the Scottish Highlands from Eighteenth to the Twentieth Centuries." *Northern Scotland* 5, 2 (1983): 99–122.

Sutton, Ann, and Richard Carr. *Tartans: Their Art and History.* New York: Arco Publishing Inc, 1984.

Taylor, Charles. *Sources of the Self: The Making of Modern Identity.* Cambridge: Cambridge University Press, 1989.

Televisionary Blog. Comment posted on 12 July 2006. http://televisionary.blogspot.com/2006/07/rewind-monarch-of-glen.html.

Telfer-Dunbar, James. *Costume of Scotland.* London: Batsford, 1981.

Thompson, E.P. *The Making of the English Working Class.* New York: Vintage, 1963.

Tölöyan, Khachig. "Rethinking Diaspora(s): Stateless Power in the Transnational Moment." *Diaspora* 5 (Spring 1996): 3–36.

Trevor-Roper, Hugh. "The Invention of Tradition: The Highland Tradition of Scotland." *The Invention of Tradition.* Ed. Eric Hobsbawm and Terence Ranger. Cambridge: Cambridge University Press, 1992.

Trumpener, Katie. *Bardic Nationalism: The Romantic Novel and the British Empire.* Princeton, NJ: Princeton University Press, 1997.

_____. "National Character, Nationalist Plots: National Tale and Historical Novel in the Age of Waverley, 1806–1830." *ELH* 60 (Autumn 1993): 685–731.

Tucker, Robert, ed. *The Marx-Engels Reader.* New York: Norton, 1978.

Turner, Adrian. *Adrian Turner on Goldfinger.* New York: Bloomsbury Publishing, 1998.

Uzell, David, ed. *Heritage Interpretation: The Natural and Built Environment.* London: Belhaven Press, 1989.

Veitch, James. *George Douglas Brown.* London: Herbert Jenkins, 1952.

Walsh, K. *The Representation of the Past: Museums and Heritage in the Post-Modern World.* London: Routledge, 1992.

Waters, Mary. *Ethnic Options: Choosing Identities in America.* Berkeley: University of California Press, 1990.

White, Hayden. *The Content of the Form: Narrative Discourse and Historical Representation.* Baltimore: Johns Hopkins University Press, 1987.

Williams, Raymond. *The Country and the City.* New York: Oxford University Press, 1973.

_____. *Marxism and Literature.* Oxford: Oxford University Press, 1977.

Withers, Charles. "Class, Culture and Migrant Identity: Gaelic Highlanders in Urban Scotland." In *Urbanizing Britain: Essays on Class and Community in the Nineteenth Century.* Ed. Charles Withers and Gerry Kearns. Cambridge: Cambridge, University Press, 1991.

_____. *Gaelic in Scotland: The Geographical History of a Language.* Edinburgh: John Donald Publishers, 1984.

_____. *Gaelic Scotland: The Transformation of a Culture Region.* London: Routledge, 1988.

Wittke, Carl. *The Irish in America.* Baton Rouge: Louisiana State University Press, 1956.

Young, Robert. *Colonial Desire: Hybridity in Theory, Culture and Race.* London: Routledge, 1995.

Yuval-Davis, Nira. *Gender and Nation.* London: Sage, 1997.

Yuval-Davis, Nira, and Floya Anthias. *Women-Nation-State.* London: Macmillan, 1989.

INDEX

Act of Union (1707) 13–14, 175, 180
Adorno, Theodor 115, 190n14
Ahmad, Aijaz 1, 20
Aidoo, Ama Ata 21–22
Allen, Theodore 21, 136, 192n81
American Scottish Coalition 114–115
Anderson, Benedict 10, 13, 20, 38, 58–59, 73, 82–83, 119, 131–132, 142, 157
Anderson, Carol 188n3
Anthias, Floya 187n68
antiquarianism 33–35, 118, 143
Arnold, Andrea 179
Arnold, Matthew 3, 6, 16, 43–46
Ashcroft, Bill 21
Auld Licht Idylls see Barrie, James

Bakhtin, Mikhail 79
Balibar, Etienne 120
Bannockburn, Batttle of (1314) 23–24, 121, 131, 154, 161
Barrie, James 7, 12, 36, 51–52, 55, 57–58, 60–62, 71, 100, 111, 155, 180
Baudrillard, Jean 115–116, 190n24
BBC Scotland 175–178
The Beatles 164
Bell, Edward 143
Bell Family Association 132–133
Benjamin, Walter 113
Beside the Bonnie Brier Bush see Maclaren, Ian
Bhabha, Homi 8, 66, 104, 153
Blair, Tony 145, 150, 152
Blake, George 28, 59
Bold, Alan 28
Boyle, Danny 12, 17, 162
Braveheart 8, 12, 115, 146–148, 152–163, 167, 176, 179–180
Brecht, Bertolt 77
Breton, Andre 77

Brigadoon 5–9, 22–23
British Heritage Act (1980) 116
Broadwood, Lucy 39
Brown, Alice 15
Brown, George Douglas 69
Brown, Gordon 180
Bruce, David 146, 150
Bruce, Duncan *see Mark of the Scot*
Burger, Peter 78, 188n15
Burns, Robert 14, 23, 73, 76, 129–130
Burns Clubs 77, 87–88, 110, 112, 129–130
Bush, George H.W. 156
The Buzzcocks 164

Campbell, J.F. 41
Canada 2, 23, 30, 37, 110, 119, 126, 128, 133, 136
Carmichael, Alexander 7–8, 39–41, 43, 47–49
Carmina Gadelica see Carmichael, Alexander
Caton-Jones, Michael 156
Celtic Revival 7–8, 39–49
Chaplin, Michael 176
Chapman, Malcolm 186n37
Clan Bell (USA) 118–119
Clan Cameron (North America) 119, 133
Clan Campbell 142
Clan Carmichael 132
Clan Donald (USA) 131, 191n69
Clan Gillespie 191n69
Clan Mackintosh 132
Clan McAlister (USA) 142
Clan Montgomery 131–132
Clan Urquhart Society 131
Clan Wallace (Worldwide) 119–120
Clifford, James 3
Cloud Howe see Gibbon, Lewis Grassic
commodity nationalism 23, 113–114, 122

203